WHEN THE STARS WHISPER

Sarah Khatib

ISBN 978-93-90463-25-1

First published in India 2022 by Leadstart Inkstate
A brand of One Point Six Technologies Pvt. Ltd.

123, Building J2, Shram Seva Premises,
Wadala Truck Terminal,
Mumbai 400022, Maharashtra, INDIA
Phone: +91 96999 33000
Email: info@leadstartcorp.com
www.leadstartcorp.com

Disclaimer: The views expressed in this book are those of the Author and do not pertain to be held by the Publisher.

Editor: Sanjhee Ginchandani
Cover: Jitendra Mahadik
Layouts: Kshitij Dhawale

i love you.

Acknowledgements

To all the dreams that were given up on too quickly, to all the dreamers who inure to their nightmares. To the stars that whisper and the broken and lost they guide.

— About the Author —

Sarah Khatib is a university student currently in pursuit of her B.A with honours in Liberal Arts. She loves everything do with the escaping reality—like every college student ever—and writing falls under that domain.

Since a young age, she has used writing as a way of expressing herself, in colourful language and in colourful ways.

Although riddled with anxiety, she has decided to take her first step towards a career in writing through the publication of her first book.

Contents

walking down memory lane

To the stars,

After the caps went up, it seemed as though the tight leash on time ceased to exist. The next few days flew by in a kaleidoscopic blur of parties and get-togethers and even though the value of those moments which everyone seemed to deem worthy of sleepless nights felt immeasurable - I didn't feel much when I cleared out those pictures from my camera roll, but, in the back of my head - I knew that all those bright memories had burned themselves in our hearts, no matter how hard we tried to deny it.

After the caps went up, it seemed as though the bullying, teasing and fist fights had never happened. All these things seemed like a whisper of conflict left in the wake of a picture-perfect class. I remember the roaring engines of cars and bikes in the parking lot - which quite frankly - got drowned by the chattering of the students, and how as each day passed, it seemed as though the same tight groups which had been formed since the beginning of time had now blended together with a strong sense of unanimity, and by the time we really got to know each other our time was up. Don't get me wrong: I don't want to go back in time to learn more about the faces that walked through the hallways and sat in my classes... that would just make saying goodbye hurt more.

After the caps went up, the sleep I once yearned for was the last thing on my mind and I found myself watching every sunrise and every sunset from my window. The sound of light and fleeting laughter replaced both the sounds of persistent and abused alarms, but, to no one's surprise, the cups of strong coffee remained a constant no matter what.

When the caps came down, we were already on our way to university where another chapter of our life would begin. We sat in planes and cars with a feeling of hope in our hearts. I looked out of the window at the dark and never-ending sky adorned with the stars waving goodbye. The blur that I called my 'high school experience' seemed good enough.

~Liberosis, Remington.

~ ✦ ~

The lone tear's companions joined him down the cheeks and to the chin of the broken boy. They came running down and they didn't seem like they were going to stop.

In his dark room, the light in his eyes began to die out and there he lay crying out to a world that passed him by – not being able to form a single coherent word. The banging on his door also seemed distant along with the voices that called out to him from the other side.

Everything felt like a distant hum.

His breathing was graduating from deep to erratic to shallow. His palms were growing clammy and were quivering. His chest became heavy like an anchor — sinking him in his mind. A white-hot pain sang through his chest and his throat began closing up while soft whimpers left his mouth.

He had the front row seat to watching his crumpled body quiver on the floor of a room which had never felt this cold. He helplessly watched the *pathetic* scene from his void. His body was no longer his and he had been reduced to a mere puppet to his anxiety.

He was shutting down.

He couldn't summon the strength to open his eyes. All he was capable of doing was watching the world around him slowly fade away.

All that surrounded him was darkness.

Through the unbreakable glass that fortified his void Malachi could see *everything* he was supposed to feel but it was locked away for *his own good*. He was safe from his emotions but deep down he knew that they would soon get to him the second he let his guard down.

It was only a matter of time. He would open his heart to the world and it would be torn apart in front him and he would retreat back into the void. However, it seemed as though there was a new breech in his in-built security system in the shape of *Remington*.

He didn't want another '*you can do it*' or '*it gets better, don't worry*'. All he wanted was to be left alone.

But to the rest of the world, that sounded like yet another cry for help.

Waking up is difficult as it is, however, waking up to a world which has no light is seemingly impossible, for in the darkness we are told to sleep.

The door to his room was locked and the knocking on the door was persistent but weakened, but he couldn't bring himself to open the door.

WEAK.
PATHETIC.

WORTHLESS.
USELESS.
WASTE OF SPACE.

A choir sang in his head. Their song relentlessly played in his head along with his echoing heartbeat. He didn't know how long he had been in the room but then again, the concept of time never made sense to him. All it did was remind him of how the world was passing him by.

He could hear the Lonely Astronaut and the North Star's familiar voices arguing on the opposite side of the door. Strangely, their muffled argument was accompanied by the warmth of comfort but their voices were a remote hum in his void of silence.

Light years away *from anything.*

He struggled to stand on his shaking legs. His clammy palms felt numb and he couldn't focus on anything. Neither the incessant banging on the door nor the tears running down his face. There were a million things running through his mind and he could not bring himself to process even a single one. They just flew by as quickly as they came and he stood there frozen and in pain. Even though this seemed better than overthinking, it didn't take the looming fear away. In that moment he was scared.

Terrified of what his mind was capable of.

The funeral was full of life, but he couldn't convince his body to get out of the house, let alone his room. His skin was translucent and it seamlessly fell into place in his black and white room.

The Lonely Astronaut and the North Star's pounding against his door was starting to sound like an off-key drum — he was surprised they hadn't knocked his door down — and even though he begrudgingly accepted every meal Mrs Mikhailov would send to his room... he couldn't taste anything.

Everything tasted like ash.

Others had also come but all their voices had blended into one, and began playing on a loop in his ears. These actions of pity fuelled his guilt and the last thing he wanted was pity. He was well aware that everyone else was in pain and grieving but they were *still* going out of their way to help *him* stand on his own two feet.

His phone made a sound and he glanced at the screen expecting another message of condolence, but instead there was a reminder.

'REMINGTON COMES BACK HOME TODAY.'

His eyes burned again.

~ ◆ ~

Words float all around us and they all have an undeniable power which grants them eternal life. This beautiful phenomenon of immortality also brings with it words which have a negative repercussion – and they too have the gift of transcending beyond life. In the shadows, lies the cold hand made of scribbled words that can make or mar the minds of those who read and hear them. The words that hurt more are the ones that were never said, for they dance on one's tongue and run rampage in their minds. *In our lives we regret more what we didn't say than what we did.*

Not knowing the repercussions of our actions and words is one of the various faults we find in the world... we do or say something being somewhat aware of the repercussions but we completely forget or ignore that and continue anyway.

He threw his phone against the wall and watched as it fell to the floor. Pieces of glass strayed from the screen which intensified the itch on his wrists.

Nothing heals, nothing ever goes back to the way it was and it probably never will. Everyone remarked that he should not have been left alone in the room but no one really had the courage to actually implement their beliefs.

He glanced at the unaddressed letter he had written, and, in that moment, he split away from every ounce of pain he had been drowning in since the accident. The pain was still there but seemingly distant – almost mocking him.

He was a puppet again and the string had yet again been tightened and his throat closed up.

He couldn't breathe.

A soft *click* sound was heard and in tip-toed two shadows. They looked at the third one lying on the floor which didn't seem at ease, even in his rare slumber. The sight of the steady yet shallow rising and falling of his chest was a relief. Satisfied, they exchanged a look and their eyes scanned the room. The letters were indeed present, *mailed* to him in fact. Set to arrive a week ago – seven days after the unbeknownst day of the accident. In the pile of envelopes, there lay a letter written in the hand of the unconscious boy.

They didn't know what to think of it.

The shadows made their way out of the room making sure to lock it again. They took comfort in knowing that they had made it through the reel of woe – that had been the last two weeks and whatever would come next could go either way.

~ ◆ ~

halo of languor

~ ✦ ~

to the stars,

do we work our best when we are all alone?

when i am at my loneliest, the whole world fades away and i still remain there standing; holding my own fragments.

i'm tired of holding them.

~idyllically, Malachi.

~ ✦ ~

Malachi couldn't afford to skip school anymore, besides, he didn't think his body was capable of crying anymore.

Getting out of his room for the first time in a little over two weeks, his legs brought him to the open kitchen and dining room where Mrs Mikhailov was calmly drizzling chocolate on waffles.

'Hi Mrs Mikhailov.' He barely whispered while fidgeting with his fingers.

She froze mid-movement and looked up to see if her ears had deceived her.

'Oh,' she seemed like she was buffering in real time, 'you are...' she trailed off taking in his lifeless form.

'Out of my room?' he offered still not looking up from his fingers.

'Yes.'

'I can't miss school anymore,' came his honest and flat reply.

In her head, she wished he was out of his room because he was feeling better even slightly.... *But at least he was out of his room.*

'The car is waiting for me.... I should probably get going.'

With that he was out of the house without sparing a second glance at the empty hallways surrounding him. It made sense that his house had a lot of glass doors and an open floor concept... sometimes the light coming from the outside substituted for the residents of the house.

He stood before the door; his hand frozen on the handle.... He could skip school for another day... it wouldn't make much of a difference any way.

He had a choice to make and he just wished someone would make it for him.

But miracles never happen and not all wishes are fulfilled.

The cool wind of the air-conditioned car hit his face the second he opened the door.

It was pleasant.

Joel did not even ask him a single question and took off the second the door was closed. The atmosphere in the car was suffocating and the uncomfortable smell of the leather seats along with their obsidian colour made his stomach churn. He felt as though he had been placed on a new planet.

The window he leaned his head against felt cold, and the drive itself felt alien.

The world seemed to fly by as the car danced through the streets. He couldn't feel a single bump in the road. The tall and dark buildings bled into the blue sky.

Splashes of colour in an otherwise plain sky.

It felt like he was watching fireworks.

The world around him felt like a canvas where he was the only thing left to be painted. He was *still* black and white in a kaleidoscopic world of colours.

It seemed as though time had passed him by and now; he was a lone soldier in a war that was over but still raged on in his head.

The silence in the car was deafening.

It was hungry and preyed on him.

Waiting for his mind to swallow him whole and then attack.

The seats were devouring him and he was waiting to get out of the car. He'd rather be lost in the winding hallways of his school adorned with strangers than be lost in his mind.

Both seemed like a labyrinth, the only difference being, one had a minotaur waiting for him on the inside and the other was empty.

The car came to a graceful halt having arrived at its destination.

Foot traffic was never something he had ever had to deal with. The private school regime had rendered his life an organised mess. The air conditioner sang through the hallways while the huge glass windows and doors let in the natural light that no one had seemed to really notice. The light hit the pale walls making them glisten, and through the hallways walked the students, all wearing something that appeared to bear a minute resemblance to the grey and blue uniform.

Noctem Arch Academy was a glorified building which pleased the eyes and promised one the comforts of a good education. It was an architectural masterpiece with its lush green lawns which were accompanied with fountains — along with its glistening gymnasiums and eccentric and free nature, but the only thing that was genuinely special about the pristine school was the library.

It was special to Malachi.

The only place in the building which had not been fortified by glass. The library was a lot like a wine cellar in an old castle. It was underground with a flooring of rustic stone matching the strong tall stone walls which supported a high ceiling, making it seem like this pocket of the pristine academy was a never-ending drop from the world upstairs. Its winding wooden and metal staircases were connected by the sturdy balconies where the wooden bookcases stood at attention. In the crevices lay wooden tables with lamps from which danced a yellow light.

Unfortunately, classes weren't held there.

They were held in the glass prison. Elegant, modern, and minimalistic rooms with only white and marble. Even the tables and chairs were a pale colour. The bright room appeared to be a well disguised interrogation room. Where everyone seemed equally guilty and went out of their way to keep a low profile.

The classes went by quickly; *too* quick for anyone to grasp anything, which in hindsight was probably why tutors were earning so much. In fact, the whole scene ran in a blur.

Malachi was fighting his own battle in his mind. He was fighting the pain in his chest while the interrogation room was getting colder by the second, and his black hoodie was rendered useless against the cold and unforgiving wind of the central air conditioner which was slipping through the fabric and marching wildly on his skin like an army without direction.

He didn't say a word. The cold was keeping him aware of where he was and stopped him from getting lost in his thoughts.

Sometimes he wondered why his grades were intact but then his mind flashed to the sleepless nights where he found himself studying to put himself to sleep.

But nothing could make Sleep whisper her enchanting spell, close his eyes and help him fall into a dreamless trance.

He was lost in his thoughts whilst walking out the door when out of nowhere a hand — a white woollen sweater paw — placed itself on his unsuspecting shoulder.

Bright.

The first word that ran through his mind was *'bright'*. He deemed the smile that greeted him worthy of such a strong word.

Bright, like a Quasar.

A voice followed the smile.

Just as jovial and bright.

'Hey, I'm Talon! I'm your partner for Mr Salone's final assignment and you've been absent,' she paused and flashed *yet another* bright smile, 'so, I thought I'd let you know.'

Talon Davis, she had transferred to Noctem Arch Academy about a year ago and had pretty much won over most of the student population.

'Oh—o-okay. I'm Malachi.' His voice felt hollow when compared to hers.

'I know!' she exclaimed, and Malachi could swear he saw actual light beaming off her, 'we can meet up in the library after school today.'

WASTE OF SPACE.

Nothing about her voice came off as suspicious or hostile — just bright.

He found himself nodding. The conversation he had with her was ringing through his head for the rest of the day and it didn't help that she was in most of his classes.

She was offbeat and bright and reeked of innocence. Malachi did not want to *taint* her.

The second the last lecture got over; Malachi found himself walking towards the library.

Bright.

She *brightly* waved at him. Her action caused her woollen white cardigan to move with her like the wings of an angel.

He reluctantly walked over to her dark corner.

'I haven't been waiting for too long so don't worry about it.' He couldn't detect anything remotely rude or cold in her chirpy voice so he begrudgingly nodded.

'So, what is the project?' he asked, sitting down and hugging his bag to his chest, fiddling with his fingers and occasionally glancing at the Quasar in front of him.

The quicker this starts the quicker it gets over.

'Yeah, we need to discuss a topic and present our perceptions of said topic, and it seems rather pointless but it is twenty-five percent of our final grade.' Her deep green eyes never left his floundering mismatched ones and somehow there was still a small smile on her face as she spoke.

'When is it due?'
'Three weeks from now since it goes on our transcripts.'
'Do you have a topic in mind?'
'We had to pick the topic from a bag.'
'What did we get?'
'People.'

Their conversation had turned into the rapid-fire round of a game show with Malachi as the reluctant host, but her final answer made him want to cry.

'Oh.' Suddenly he didn't want to have anything to do with the project.

Malachi didn't know if the Quasar in front of him had noticed the change in his tone or the way that he flinched when she answered his question. Well... maybe she did... but she just didn't care.

NOBODY CARES.

'Furthermore, every step of the project has to be done together and agreed upon,' she continued on in her same chirpy tone.

'How about we make the topic revolve around our connections to people and the entire concept of human lives and their relationships?' He nodded noting that the Quasar in front of him had a plan written in stone. It *almost* seemed like the last clause of the project had hindered her from all but finishing it, while Malachi was trapped in his mind and locked away in his room.

A slow discussion on the way they would move about the whole project began. Her bright smile only held warmth; something he had not seen or even felt in a long time.

After an hour of discussing they came to a consensus.

'So, we will be writing a joint essay which will have three elements,' she began reading from her laptop screen which made her earthen eyes gleam like an untouched forest.

'Firstly, pictures of people doing something that brings a smile to their faces. Their reason as to why it brings them joy... and?' She looked back at him to continue.

'How these things connect us as people and if these things are caused by other people,' he finished calmly while squeezing his bag closer to his chest.

He would have to spend way more time with her than he had originally anticipated.

'I have a really good feeling about this,' she chirped while packing her stuff up.

'I'm free most of tomorrow so we can click the pictures then... are you free tomorrow? I don't want you to miss your lectures.'

Malachi questioned the concern but brushed it off.

'I only have math in the morning,' he supplied.

'Great! Me too,' she practically sang with glee, 'do you have a camera that you can bring?'

Malachi blinked slowly.

Yes, Malachi had a camera. *Remington* had gifted him one before he left for university and in return Malachi would send him a picture a day — he used to send him pictures of everything under the sun that he was drawn to. But the phone calls and messages stopped after a month and the pictures lasted for two.

'A camera will have a better result than a phone,' she quickly justified.

'Yes, I have one.'

'Don't forget it!' She smiled, and with that they made their way out of the library and towards the school gate... which quite frankly was calling out to him. He could see the front of his car and quickened his pace with his vision narrowing onto the hood of the car.

The Quasar wasn't even taken aback by his erratic behaviour.

She didn't even ask him a single question.

'Malachi!' A strong, new but awfully familiar voice called.

He didn't bother to turn around and muttered a soft farewell to no one in particular and threw himself into his car. He just wanted to be left alone.

But miracles never happen and not all wishes are fulfilled.

~ ✦ ~

enigmatic silence

To the stars,

The concept of judging people is useless. They say 'don't judge a book its cover.' Yet that is what most us find ourselves doing. If you don't appear beautiful then you aren't made for this world. That is the sad truth, one will only try to learn about your personality if they are taken by your appearance.

That, or you have to be unrealistically talented and then years later they will use you as a new definition of beauty; 'unique' or 'unconventional' are the terms that will be used. Maybe we all are someone else's definition of beautiful or another flowery adjective like that but I don't see a need to hold out hope for myself. What is there is there and what isn't, isn't.

I find university to be a maze of falling into one web from another in hopes of breaking free from the sticky and seemingly beautiful confines of the trap before, the spider reaches the victim. The concept of beauty being given more credit serves a larger purpose in university that I expected.

~Liberosis, Remington.

~ ✦ ~

Malachi looked positively zapped.

Had he somehow attained a new *friend*? Looking up from his coffee — courtesy of Mrs Mikhailov — and at the girl with flowing golden hair, who sat in front of him merrily munching on her granola bar while her eyes scanned the screen of her laptop. She looked up from her laptop and turned the screen around to face him. He found himself being greeted by various open sticky notes that were over-flowing with tasks which caused him to gawk at her with concern painted on his soft features.

'We need to make a list of people we will be interviewing,' she said with a smile and went back to munching on her snack, and it was at that exact moment, ladies and gentlemen, that his eyes found an empty sticky note titled *'Final Grade: Project.'*

Right, that's why she was sitting with him.

WHY WOULD SOMEONE EVER WANT TO BEFRIEND YOU?

'Do you have anyone in mind?' *The quicker this starts the quicker this gets over.*

'Not really,' she shrugged, 'I was thinking we could go by the clubs and find people to interview there.'

That was a good idea.

He nodded.

'We could start with the music club... that's usually full of life right now,' he offered.

Bright.

She nodded and quickly began packing up.

'I know it's not my place to ask you this, but why weren't you coming to school for like two weeks?'

'Personal problems.' After noticing the evident change in her facial expression, he quickly added, 'I don't want to elaborate.'

She reluctantly nodded as they walked past a group of loud people.

A 'Hey Talon!' sounded unanimously from the group.

'Hey guys! How've you been?' She stopped walking and spoke to them for a few minutes like she was genuinely interested in their lives.

Malachi found himself zapped yet again.

What fresh hell was this? How can a person be this nice to so many people?

She was like the sun and everyone was moving around her.

Only she was brighter and more powerful.

He knew most of the people in that group because of his parents' social circles and events which were buzzing spots for small talk, which Malachi did not care for.

He offered a tight-lipped smile which was returned almost instantly.

While the Quasar wrapped up her conversations Malachi's hands began to feel heavy. He hadn't been *there* in so long and he didn't even know why he'd suggested this place. He had surprised the both of them when he gave the suggestion. While they continued walking through the cold hallway again, his body was working on autopilot to get him *there,* and the second he stepped out into the garden the warmth froze his skin.

The members of the music club were seated *outside* the music club room in their usual spot – under the willow tree with the occasional visits from the members of the art club. Whenever the talent of the art club had heated arguments — which was quite frequently — the distraught members would escape to the hidden realm under the Willow tree. They all seemed to fall into place together, hidden and protected by the tree.

The soft and soothing notes of the lyre and violin sang mysteriously in the garden. The students who stood around the fountain had their eyes closed and were gently swaying to the music. While many ran around in groups enjoying the sun and the atmosphere around them with lively smiles, as they unknowingly made memories to last a lifetime.

In the afternoon when the light hits the tree the hidden garden turns into something out of a fairytale. The soft wind blows the leaves and their green curtain dances to the music.

Nature's symphony.

The art club stood with their canvases and messy clothes. Flecks of paint littered their clothes, hands, and faces.

He remembered the day everyone stayed back in school to do last-minute work for a school festival, and under the night sky hidden in the tree sat the art and music club. They were taking a break and everyone found themselves gathered around the disguised angels.

The winds were soft.
The night was cool.
The stars were bright.

And in that moment the whole school was in a trance.

Aurora Borealis.

Magical.
Mystical.
Musical.

Mahnoor Rafiq was on the lyre while Nuriyah Rafiq played the violin.

Breathtaking.
Beautiful.
Bewitching.

Upon reaching the Willow tree, Malachi and the Quasar's eyes landed on the disguised angels who were in a trance themselves.

The violin was singing.

Her mellifluous voice was ineffable.
Nuriyah's movements were precise and calculated, but free.

The lyre's sonorous notes were hypnotic.
Mahnoor's fingers danced.
Lingering.

They were having a conversation in an ancient dialect.

Nature's Symphony.

Malachi snapped a picture.

The mahogany-eyed twins stopped and looked at the source of the sound.

In the background he could see a familiar figure.
'...Malachi,' Nuriyah murmured.
He nodded at her in acknowledgement.

'We're so sorry to interrupt you but we need your help with our project,' the Quasar's bubbly voice filtered through the warm air.

'Sure, how can we help you?' the violinist asked in her smooth voice.
'We need an interview with the two of you.'
'About?'
'Your passion and how it attained such a place in your life.'
'Ahhhh.'

Steadying his hands with a deep breath Malachi signalled the Aurora Borealis and began recording.
'Hi. My name is Mahnoor Rafiq.'
'And mine is Nuriyah Rafiq.'

'When we were first brought to our adoptive parents, we couldn't speak any English... so along with our language classes we were taught to play instruments.'

She paused and Nuriyah continued seamlessly.

'We couldn't really communicate with them but when we played pieces for them, we could see the joy in their eyes as they watched us and that helped us convey our feeling and thoughts.'

'We love them and that's how we showed it.'

'Yeah... and it helped us connect with others, and in school it helped us make friends... in a way music saved us.'

'Yeah, and even now whenever they play people stop by to listen and their joy is shared.' The figure in the background called out.

Acenath Delia Genevieve Simmons; she sat with her back pressed against the trunk of the tree. Her hands were moving rapidly as she sketched something. Her previously natural black hair represented the colours of the rainbow and her black eyes trained themselves on her paper.

Malachi snapped a picture of the new speaker in her element even though he probably had albums of such pictures.

'Don't try to interview me.'
'I won't even bother,' he sounded back.

They'd known each other since the beginning of time and he still couldn't bring himself to call the pastel rainbow-haired girl his friend.

'It's good to see you back at school.'
'I'm surprised you even noticed the lack of me.'
'Please! How do you think all your assignments and classwork even reached your house? Courtesy of me.'

She sprung to her feet and walked over to him with her sketch book in hand.

A hug.

Comfort. A space station to an astronaut, but in reality, she herself was the Lonely Astronaut lost in space.

'I'm sorry,' she whispered as he clung onto her.
He couldn't bring himself to call his cousin his friend.
She was so much more.

~ ◆ ~

The Quasar had been thrown off by an important submission that had *just* come up and was rather busy. With their finals slowly approaching the teachers were throwing random hurdles their way every few days. Meanwhile, Malachi spent the rest of the day in the library. He sat there covering up all the stuff that he had missed over that past two weeks. He plugged his earphones into his laptop and inhaled deeply at the soft serene notes of the piano, taking a deep breath. for what was about to happen next.

And not even a second later, there she was in all her glory.

Kamaria.

She sat beside him with her long and messy hair which seemed like they could defy gravity. She wore a white sundress which complemented the black and grey vines tattooed on her right arm. Her blunt nails picked at the soft fabric of her dress incessantly, while her eyes contrasted the colour of the dress and matched her rebellious hair. When the light hit her eyes you could see the warm brown separate itself from her pupil and her signature smile.

Her smile hid a lot.

In Malachi's eyes she looked like a child of nature.

'It's been a long time hasn't it?' Her honeyed voice laced with concern made a shiver run down his spine.

'It has... I couldn't bring myself to touch a piano.'
'You couldn't bring yourself to leave your room.'

A fact, painful nonetheless.

'You've been talking to people.'
'Yeah... it's tiring... I need a break; it's all too much,' he brushed off the

insinuation of her statement and began going through his never-ending list of assignments.

She hummed again.

'You've grown.'
'Barely.'

She raised an eyebrow at him but brushed off his cold behaviour, she was used to it.

'They care about you.'
'I don't know why.'
'Are they wrong to do that?'

'They aren't right,' he all but whined, 'there are so many things wrong with me,' he huffed and his voice fell to a whisper. 'And they are going to get hurt.'
'Nobody is flawless,' she stated matter-of-factly, 'they are aware of the consequences.
'I don't want to-'
'You promised the stars, didn't you?' There it was, the ultimate blow.

Malachi stopped talking and tore his eyes away from his laptop screen and piling work.

'I don't want to hurt them,' he muttered, 'not again.'
'You won't.'

He scoffed at the confidence in her voice.

~ ✦ ~

Malachi continued working after Kamaria took her leave and found himself drowning in the silence of the library. He couldn't bring himself to break to the surface and relieve his burning lungs. The water was cold and dark, he could see the light fading and he felt himself get heavier and heavier as he sunk to the bottom.

His lungs felt heavy and his palms were getting sweatier as the seconds passed. His thoughts were running rampage.

He wasn't alone, he was alone with his thoughts.

The room grew colder and the air got thicker.

'get yourself together.'
FREAK.
'breathe.'
WASTE OF SPACE.
'close your eyes.'
USELESS.
FAILURE
WEAK.
'don't listen to them.'

Malachi was trapped in the freezing current.

'breathe, count to five.'
'come on, Malachi.'

'that's it.'
'there you go'
'you are okay.'

Malachi surfaced with an aching chest.

He glanced at his watch.

'Great... twenty minutes lost,' he muttered in disdain.

Malachi went on working quietly, with his thoughts all over the place.

His wrists were itching.

His mind flashed back to the first time he decided to do something about the incessant itching.

~ ◆ ~

Thirteen-year-old Malachi was lying in bed wondering how he'd survived.
He'd made sure that the cuts were deep.
Yet, here they were — stitched up — he assumed, and wrapped up tightly by a white bandage.
He was tired, it had been two weeks since the *incident* and now he was laying on his bed watching the sun rise.

But now, the sun had set.

He was slowly became aware of the bustling behind the doors but he couldn't bring himself to care, if anything it sounded like a repetitive screech. However, another distinct sound stood out to him.

It sounded familiar

And it was persistent and consistent.
Through the fog in his mind Malachi registered it as a piano. He was so busy trying to place the sound that he didn't realise that a hand had slipped into his.

'I'm Kamaria. It's nice to meet you Malachi.'

Malachi, although dazed, nodded in acknowledgement. *Remington.* And with just one name everything came rushing back into his dazed mind. 'He doesn't hate you,' she offered with a soft smile, but her words meant nothing to him.

Malachi slipped further into the fleeting warmth of his blankets.

He didn't know how to face him, what to say or even what to do.
'He will yell at me,' his voice sounded scratchy.
'Well that's because he cares,' she gently squeezed his hand. 'That's because they all care.'

'I hurt them.'

She smiled sadly at him and gently tugged him towards her.
'You didn't hurt them, you hurt yourself.'
The unsaid words danced in the air while the girl with the honeyed voice helped the obsidian-haired boy out of the bed. Fortunately for her, the boy was too dazed to notice what she was doing.

'He'll be better off without me.'

His words hurt her, but they didn't deter her.
'He can be the judge of that.'
'I don't want to hurt them,' he whispered while she made him stand on his feet.
'Then don't hurt yourself,' she whispered and guided him in his first step.

'Go to him.'

'Why would he — wait!! Where are you taking me?' Even after realising that she was leading him to the source of the music itself, his body followed her. They were making their way down the stairs and the music was getting louder and clearer.
Malachi felt overwhelmed.

'Where are Acenath and Devon?'

She smiled in response and continued to the lead him to the piano. it was then when Malachi realised, she had black and grey vines tattooed all over her right arm that lead him.
She gestured to the couch where Malachi could see the duo lying supine. Malachi could merely see the outlines of their figures from the distance but he knew it was them. Next to them sat his parents, with their heads in their hands.

'I can't,' he gasped.
He couldn't move any further, his feet grew roots into the marble floor and his heart began to sink.
She noticed the colour drain from his face but she didn't want to delay the inevitable.
'Malachi, don't be afraid, they love you.'
'That will be their demise.'
Although his pessimistic attitude hurt her, she didn't show it.

'That's up to you.'

'You have their hearts in your hands Malachi, it's all up to you.'
Show the world that you care about them.
'Why do you think they are still here?'

'Obligation, guilt, and pity,' he listed off the top of his head.

'Love, Malachi, love.'

'You are worth their love and so much more.'
I'm not.'
'You are. You just don't know it yet,' she shrugged and pulled him towards
the piano.
Malachi recognised the melancholic tune and his eyes burned.

'Remington - I -' But before he could finish the sentence, the white-haired
pianist's fingers froze along with the rest of his body and he slowly turned
around to face the obsidian-haired boy. His eyes bore into Malachi's, who
couldn't look away from the familiar pools of darkness.

Tears.

They ran down the white-haired boy's face profusely while Malachi watched
helplessly.
He didn't know what to do, but the decision was already made for him.
Remington leaned forward and pulled Malachi towards him and sobbed into
his chest.

He was wasting his tears.

Alerted by the sobs and the abrupt halt to the music, his parents, Acenath
and Devon, rushed over to the duo by the piano and in their embrace,
Malachi cried helplessly, but he wasn't the only one.
'Don't ever do that,' Acenath managed between her broken sobs.
Malachi nodded frantically.
'Promise me, Malachi,' Remington added looking up at the obsidian-haired
boy.

'I promise.'

'Malachi, they love you,' she said with a knowing smile 'You just need to see
that.'
With that Kamaria was gone, but Malachi knew she would be back.

never-ending amalgamation of failing hypothesis

To the stars,

'Ignorance is bliss'. Whoever said that had an impenetrable mental, emotional, and physical barricade built. Somehow the statement or rather an observation made by said person does not serve to be true in my life. Anytime I ignore something it snowballs into a ginormous concoction of awaiting doom.

I know my words aren't making any sense right now but the overview of said concern can be a proved hypothesis is my life. Exhibit A: I *ignored* the ingredients in my medicine which resulted in an allergy attack, which resulted in my missing a math test, which lead to my teacher humiliating me with the audience of my entire class.

Similarly, it has helped in other situations. Exhibit B: I *ignored* the fight between my neighbours and got a fruit and muffin basket from both (they were trying to win me over). Rendering the development of my hypothesis absolutely useless, I'm not making my own decisions anymore and neither am I existing on the basis of my desires.

I feel like all I am doing is proving someone else's theories.

~Liberosis, Remington.

~ ✦ ~

While the days passed him by Malachi was pleasantly surprised that he had managed to cover up a little over a week's worth of work with the amount of chaos around him. The usually quiet library shared an uncanny resemblance with a zoo. At any given time, various people were running in and out like headless chickens desperately searching for books that they usually walked past, but now with their exams approaching the library was where most of the student population ended up to *feel* productive. They were all lying to themselves. It's not like they were going to get any work done and everything was getting set aside for *later*… whenever that was.

Malachi wrapped up his work and decided to end the day earlier than he had planned. He walked through the people around him, desperate to get to his car.

He didn't feel anything.
He felt numb.

He felt empty, but he welcomed this feeling because even though it wasn't pleasant or even comfortable it was better than his frequenting panic attacks. He would happily settle for the lesser of the two evils but due to this new feeling he was not only numb to his emotions but also to the world around him. His indifferent attitude raised red flags in the minds of the people who could see the change in his eyes. But how could they bring this up when he walked right through them?

Malachi was fortified. Closed off, now more than ever.

The numbing ache in his chest was slowly eating him and he didn't know how to deal with it… but it was better than spending the whole day crying and losing to his mind. What he had recently realised was that there was a fear that came with the pain. It wasn't the fear of the pain itself because he was used to it. He had learned how to numb himself to it but recently this pain had grown stronger. A pain to which he's not numb too.

It started off as a rare spike but now it was becoming an everyday occurrence.

This is what created the fear.

Not the fact that the pain existed.
But, the fear of *what if.*
The fear of the pain getting worse.

What if the pain gets worse and he learns to become numb to that as well?
What if this creates a pattern?
What if he can't cope with it?

These fears fed Hope, igniting her flame, but like a double-edged sword it paved the way for the voices.

~ ✦ ~

Malachi loved photography.

He often found the world passing him by.

So, he found his own coping mechanism in photography. He liked to have pieces of the brighter moments in his hands. Sometimes, the darkness blinded him from seeing the light that had once flourished around and within him.

In the end, the brighter moments are reminisced, not the moments when you lay broken and helpless on the floor but those lows help you appreciate the flashes of uncontrollable laughter and warm comfort. The lows dance around in the back of your head almost like a reminder of your strength and who you are and how you've gotten there. The fragments get swept under the turning pages that mark the beginning and end of a new chapter, and he was just entering adulthood.

How long until they're all memories?

Malachi couldn't sleep with his mind running a mile a minute, and he couldn't keep up with it but he didn't have a choice.

He braced himself for the rollercoaster of emotions he was going to

memory

Taking my breath away,
wanting to stay, day after day.
Making your place in my mind.
I don't know what to do with your kind
Like an endless burden in my head.
Please stop, don't talk, can't you wait till I'm dead.

Memory, you've painted pictures in my head.
Your burning flame fills me with dread.
Colours so bright, you bring me to plight.
Burning with a flame of the darkest light.
Life is a game I fail to fight.
Please stop, don't talk, can't you see I'm scared.

Just wait until I'm dead.

Can't you see I'm ripped and broken.
Memory, you've taken your final token.

~ ✦ ~

tactical advantages and technical glitches

To the stars,

I blinded myself into believing that as humans and technology have evolved, it was supposed to get easier for us to connect with each other, but now this has entirely backfired and it is easier to ignore a person through the various means of social media and other sources of technology.

I know exactly where to go to accidently run into people and how to get away from them. The convenience of it is now mundane.

Somehow, I still can't find you.

~Liberosis, Remington..

~ ◆ ~

The day was too long — waiting for the football club to get done with practice was seemingly longer — simply put, they were *too* passionate about it. A perfect time to take a picture, however their passion came out on the same wavelength.

The mismatched duo couldn't bring themselves to decide.

They were like meteorites, flying streaks of passion running across their universe — and quite frankly — they didn't look very approachable.

Malachi and the Quasar didn't know who in their right mind would even try to interrupt them whatsoever.

Yet here they were, getting ready to interrupt them.

The world on the field was chaotic, yet everything seemed in order while the ball seemed to fly everywhere – hopefully not into the bystanders' faces. The players were gliding on the field but their movements weren't even close to graceful. They only appeared to have one objective and that was to win.

Malachi found it quite amusing that they honed their skills by fighting against their own teammates.

'Watch out!!' A deep but awfully familiar voice called out and Malachi's instant reaction was to move away from the voice.

Far, far, away.

This however, rendered his face in the way of a very fast-moving ball – skin – that is the first thing that flashed before his eyes. A leg – effectively deflected the ball.

'What part of *watch out* did you not get?' The familiar deep voice getting closer and sounding more agitated while the never-ending game paused itself, and soon all the players were surrounding them. While Malachi wanted the ground to swallow him whole — with all sets of eyes on him, the Quasar wasn't intimidated. Not even at the slightest.

Bright.

Malachi turned to the owner of the leg, a boy with deep red, dyed hair.

The Meteorite who didn't seem fazed whatsoever.

'Thank you,' Malachi barely managed to get the words out and continued fidgeting with his fingers almost refusing to meet the eyes of the Meteorite.

'Don't mention it Malachi.' He practically hissed his name.

'You can't ignore me forever.' The human Moral Compass called out.

Malachi could try.

'Hey guys we were-'Malachi zoned out while the Quasar explained their project to the meteorites that surrounded them.

He didn't bring his eyes to meet the Moral Compass;' he just couldn't bring himself to do that.

Why did they have to talk to the football club? There are many more people in the school, so why the football club? The pictures of the swimming and diving team would be way cooler – water is always beautiful *and* he didn't know anyone in those clubs. The group project was turning out to be a bigger nightmare than he had anticipated.

'-Malachi? Malachi? Are you okay?'

'Yes.' The mechanical lie flew out of his mouth instantly.

'They've started their game,' she smiled gesturing to the game before them, 'do you want to start clicking pictures?' Her question left him wondering how long he had zoned out for.

'Yeah.'

He looked at the meteorites who were back in action. They didn't look *that* terrifying from a distance.

The game was quick and their movements were erratic; there was too much chaos.

In the blink of an eye the game could change. The match was only friendly in name. All the meteorites were in sync, moving on instinct, and commands flew out of the meteorites' mouths occasionally and even after falling they sprung back up in action. The sounds of the movement resembled an army. When the ball is with a player, they're not only aware of their own movements but also aware of their close surroundings. Afterall, the more observant the player the better the player.

And that's when it happened.

The ball flew up after striking against one of the meteorite's legs and a dark streak of red ran towards the ball meeting it mid-air. The ball zipped to the goal and the meteorite came to the ground.

The game was over.

The moment was ephemeral.

Malachi snapped a picture.

Water is beautiful. However, the picture that greeted him on the LCD screen was in a league of its own. There stood the red flame back on the ground. Giving the mismatched duo a lopsided grin, he began to walk over.

'Can we finish off the interview now?' His question was direct.

The more observant the player, the stronger they are.

~ ✦ ~

The mismatched duo was staring at the picture, in fact, neither of them had even acknowledged the lean meteorite in front of them.

'Guys?' The Moral Compass called out.

Malachi's head instantly snapped up and he inched away from The Moral Compass.

'Yeah,' she chirped, 'Malachi are you ready?' The Quasar's voice sounded distant.

'Ready.'

'Okay, let's begin.'

Malachi began recording.

'Hi, my name is Vince Mafler and you clicked a picture of me in my element,' he flashed yet another lopsided grin, 'it's not the thing that necessarily brings me joy.'

Malachi and The Quasar shared a look.

'I don't think anything can bring undeniable joy,' he paused, 'the air is full of excitement, and a sense of belonging I learnt by playing with my brother and my father,' he smiled fondly at the memory. I remember watching the older kids playing and their determination to win. Thinly veiled by their innocent smiles.'

'I've made most of my friends through this game. Yeah, it changed my life but its impact wasn't that big. It taught me patience and the importance of teamwork,'
He paused *almost* for dramatic effect, 'more importantly, it got me addicted to the taste of victory.'

Malachi ended the recording.

'Great! Good luck with your project.'
With that he launched back to the rest of the meteorites.

They walked away from the field.

'What the hell just happened?' Malachi blurted out.
'Dude!! You're asking me? I'm pretty sure I would have died if I had to play against him,' she tipped her head back laughing. 'My limbs would have detached themselves from my body if I went anywhere near that ball.'

Back to silence.

'Do you think that was enough for today?'
'Yeah.'

Malachi had a sick feeling that the project was going to take way longer than planned because of the wide array of eccentric interviewees.

'Is it just me or does it seem like everyone is hell-bent on ruining our project with their unconventional answers?' She began laughing at her own observation and Malachi cracked a smile having thought of the same thing.

Yup, the Quasar was back to normal.

The walk was quiet and long. The grounds were quite a walk from the main building. A beautiful walk nonetheless. The grass was well maintained and the cobblestone walkway was striking as always, every single corner of the institution was beautiful and elegant. Making the whole experience feel ethereal, but the trauma the students left with balanced out the beauty of the institution.

Malachi was so absorbed in his surrounding that he barely registered someone calling out his name in the distance.

'-ALACHI! MALACHI?'

'MALACHI! WAIT UP.' The Lonely Astronaut with the Meteorite in tow made their way to them – *a strange pair* – they stopped, waiting for them to catch up.

'Hello!' The Quasar chirped waving her cardigan-clad arm.
The Lonely Astronaut waved her charcoal covered hand in return and the Meteorite nodded in acknowledgement.

Back to silence.
They continued walking.

'I know it's not my place but why have you been ignoring Devon?'
'Funny story,' the Lonely Astronaut supplied.

'Is it really?' The Meteorite chipped in while running his hand through his hair.
'It soon will be,' she glared at him. 'It's also a story for another time,' the Lonely Astronaut shot back.

'I could just ask him.' The Meteorite evidently had a death wish.

The Quasar nodded her head in support.

'Nope. You guys like me more.'
'How are you so sure?' The Quasar chirped in.
'Because I have met Devon.'

'...Touché.'
'Yeah, she makes a point.'

The Quasar and the Meteorite murmured.

Malachi felt warm.
Not because of the sun.

The Lonely Astronaut.
The Quasar.
The Meteorite.

'MALACHI ELAKRAB!!!!'

And the fast-approaching Moral Compass, *the man of the hour himself.*

The Lonely Astronaut and Malachi shared a look.

'If we run, we can get to your car in time.'
'That seems pointless.'
'Yeah, because of these two.'

The Quasar and the Meteorite gave the duo a look.

'We are right here,' the Quasar said matter-of-factly.
'And?'
'We can hear you,' the Meteorite offered.
'So?'
'So? You know what-'

'I'll just get it over with.' Malachi interrupted the three of them while staring at his black Converse.

He didn't like conflict.

'Are you sure?'

'Yeah.'

The Moral Compass was getting closer now.

His expression didn't give away much, but by the way he was huffing and puffing, one could almost see the steam coming out of his ears.

He came to a stop right in front of them.

'Hello again Johnson,' the Meteorite called out, 'love the new haircut,' gesturing to the muscular teen's high-low fade.

Was he stalling?
Why was he stalling?

The others all offered a wave.

'Malachi, we need to talk.'
'I know.'

'How about coffee after school today?'
'Yeah but-'

'I will be there as well,' the Lonely Astronaut announced; her tone held a sense of finality.
'Sure.'

~ ✦ ~

His car didn't feel empty.
Joel felt like things were finally going back to normal.
Malachi had his eyes glued to the world outside the car.

It looked better without him on the canvas.
He was still black and white in a kaleidoscopic world of colours.

~ ✦ ~

happy ever after

To the stars,

I don't really like this world; we all say that the world is on the grey scale but that is merely an excuse.

In reality, everything is subjective to such an extent that there is not only the grey scale but also the various other colour scales that come into the picture of our world.

You get saved from this minefield of mayhem but some colours can be felt.

~Liberosis, Remington.

~ ✦ ~

The coffee shop is its own universe. It has its own environment and ecosystem. In there you can't smell the smoke and madness of the outside world; only the indulgent aroma of coffee. When one walks in through the huge glass doors; they are greeted by the soft, aromatic, and cool wind.

Everyone in the coffee shop functions on their own tangent. On one table, teenagers with their laptops and books out — desperately trying to convince themselves (and others around them) that they are *indeed* doing work. On another, adults sipping coffee, working on their laptops at a quick pace — almost desperate to leave. On a table in the middle of all the typing and laughter, is a tired parent with a child who is bouncing off the walls, another may have a young couple on a date and friends catching up.

The coffee shop has huge glass windows and three floors; a basement and a terrace seating, however the area where the heavenly drinks themselves are made has no seating whatsoever, probably so that the basristas can work in silence? Nobody is quite sure; while some see it as a waste of space most can't bring themselves to care.

The coffee shop itself is rather mismatched. With a rustic theme and rather sophisticated furniture, accompanied by the open floor plan makes it feel more spacious.

It reminds Malachi of the library, after all they do have a similar design.

The terrace is very different all together, the picnic-style tables under the huge umbrellas make it look a lot like a beach-front property. The terrace looks very beautiful, however the sweltering environment created by the burning sun chars anything and everything. However, there are always people present here with colder drinks which have extravagant names and sunglasses, clicking pictures, whiling away their time. It didn't make sense to the bystanders but it was their little vacation so no one questioned it.

The basement on the other hand is a very different place. Not a single picnic table in sight. Only comfy sunken couches with bean bags and low-lying coffee tables. There was however one community table on which all those with laptops and small cups of coffee sat at. Malachi often saw people from his school at the coffee shop. They all came to the coffee shop like moths to a flame.

The walls were all sunken in bookshelves with dusty books which had probably never been read since they had been placed there, whatever part of the wall was visible looked a lot like a cave and the celling followed the same pattern.

After getting their coffee the trio made their way to the basement.

Silence.

Malachi wondered how long it would last for.

'Why do you need such a complicated coffee order?' The Moral Compass asked with a scowl.
'Because,' The Lonely Astronaut shrugged off his question.
'That just inconveniences the barista.'
'But my coffee is made just for me then.'
'Isn't that just selfish?'
'Nope, it's just me training them to deal with the various types of customers.'
'If you don't give an extravagant order, you'll lessen their burden.'

The Lonely Astronaut and the Moral Compass had already started bickering – they weren't even seated. While the Moral Compass didn't see the need for her presence but if this is how he could talk to Malachi, it was a price he was willing to pay.

No one uttered a word as they made their way to one of the couches. They were contently sipping their drinks and Malachi found himself wary of the peaceful atmosphere around them. It was almost too peaceful.

The second everyone found their place the Moral Compass cleared his throat.

'We haven't even made ourselves comfortable.'
'I'm so sorry I didn't take your comfort into account.'

'You should be.'
'Are you comfortable now?'

'Yup!'
'Okay then- '
'You didn't ask Malachi.'

The Moral Compass was used to the Lonely Astronaut's behaviour but he still couldn't help but roll his eyes.

'Malachi are you comfortable?' His deep voice sounded saccharine-sweet and devoid of emotion.

'With you around that would be impossible.' The Lonely Astronaut was ignored.

She was trying her best to delay the inevitable.

'Malachi... did you get the letters as well?'
He froze.

'Yeah,' he swallowed thickly, 'I got the letters.'
'Ace?' she mutely reached into her bag.

Did the others also get letters?
He thought he was the only one.

Jay was dressed in his dark green trench coat that sat well on his black button-up and black pants. On his luscious black and messy hair with a few green streaks sat his beanie. His eyes matched his trench coat flickering with amusement, but his smirk was sinister. Malachi wanted him to leave, but instead he sat right next to him. Looking upon the conversation with a childish smile. His elbows rested on his knees and he placed his head in his hands.

Malachi wanted him to leave.
He didn't want him there.

'They got letters as well Lily,' his eyes held Malachi's, 'and you thought you were the closest to Eros Remington.' His voice was velvety but his words hurt — because Malachi knew they were true.

Malachi ignored him. He *tried* to ignore him and pay attention to the Moral Compass and the Lonely Astronaut, but their voices were muffled and distant and he couldn't look away from *him*.

He was underwater.
He was drowning.
He could see their mouths moving.

His chest hurt and he felt the sudden urge to cry.

'I guess I should leave,' he pouted. 'This was a useless visit,' Jay got up, 'take care of yourself Lily,' he gave Malachi his dimpled smile and left.

Just as mysteriously and quickly as he had come.

Why did he leave?

'Malachi?' The Lonely Astronaut's muffled voice called out.
The duo in front of him were holding out envelopes.

Letters.

'Malachi? You okay?'
'Yeah,' he continued, 'I'm okay.' His voice came out raspy.

'I'm sorry I didn't give them to you earlier,' she closed her eyes. 'I didn't know how you'd react.' The Lonely Astronaut's voice was laced with guilt and her eyes flickered to the Moral Compass.

Wait... why would they give the letters to him?

'We didn't read them.'
A blatant lie.
They all knew it.

'They came to us in the mail on the day of the...' she trailed off.
Funeral.
The unsaid word rang clearly.

'We couldn't get in touch with you,' he whispered, 'so we waited.'
'Malachi,' she whispered reaching for his hand. 'I'm sorry I didn't tell you earlier — I-I should have just listened to Devon.'

I wanted to protect you.

The Lonely Astronaut knew that the North Star was right — they can't protect him forever.

The North Star was rarely ever wrong and *people always run away from the truth.*

Malachi held the letters in his shaky hands.
They were all addressed to him.

Malachi felt his self-defence system sound the alarm and Malachi ran away from the coffee shop and to his car.

He was going home.

If he could call it that.

~ ✦ ~

Malachi never really saw his parents as humans. He knew they were good at what they did and probably loved what they did but he would know more about them if they spoke to each other. His parents are powerful individuals with charismatic personalities that somehow ended up with each other. The one thing that they had in common is the fact that they usually forget that they are human.

Malachi loves them.
But then again, he doesn't *know* them.

While Malachi looked like his mother, they both had the same smile, wispy built and thick dark locks – the only difference being that there is a light in her eyes and her smile is always present.

The Elakrab family pushes itself to no end.
They forget that they are human.

Malachi gave his parents a soft greeting while they were on their phones on important calls. It's not that they didn't care about each other. They had just developed a system to make sure that they could all benefit from and live their own individual lives.

Then again, the system of the world is broken and this system was heading the same way.

~ ✦ ~

everything is falling apart into place

To the stars,

I find myself staying up when I should be sleeping. The night calls out to me — technically the grand piano calls out to me and as it turns out, I have an audience.

The library is pretty close to the piano and the windows are open at one thirty on the dot when I begin to play.

I don't yearn for sleep anymore.

I find myself staying awake for nights on end. It's usually me and coffee... until last week.

I made a friend.

A fellow insomniac and coffee addict, and since she's a law student, this all works out for her. Technically she's studying criminology. But I don't want to get into the technicalities. She is the first person I have met here who is not from this island that once ruled the world.

She insists on meeting you... how can I tell her that I can't grow a spine and talk to you?

She plans on stealing your number and messaging you — so I'm warning you for what it's worth.

You'd love her. She's honest and the embodiment of reality.

She works hard and speaks five languages and claims to get confused easily between these languages, but in reality, she pulls you in with her words and there you stay.

She's from Seoul and no matter how hard she tries to hide it that's where her heart will always be.

~Liberosis, Remington.

~ ✦ ~

The week flew by too quickly, in Malachi's opinion. Probably because he spent most of his time working on the project and running away from any confrontation. He felt more out of place than usual and the world was passing him by more often than not, and he had a new problem.

The Quasar.

He didn't have a problem with *her*... but he was finding it difficult to dodge her, and no matter how much he tried to push her away with his empty and short responses she wouldn't budge. He wondered if she thought of him as a *charity case.* Most people were put off by his cold behaviour but she found the way he fidgeted with his fingers when nervous and the way he held his bag to his chest, *endearing.* In which world was Malachi Elakrab endearing?

It didn't help that the Lonely Astronaut and the North Star were always hovering around him.

CHARITY CASE.

They were both outgoing people and had *friends*, yet here they were with Malachi. Sometimes he wondered why they'd stuck around after so many years but he knew why they stuck around.

It's because too much had happened between them and they were too stubborn to become strangers again.

Malachi was desperate to maintain a low profile but as he had recently learnt, the Lonely Astronaut and the Meteorite were closer than ever and were more of a package deal than anything.

So, with the pastel-haired girl who perpetually had flecks of paint or charcoal smudges littering her face and hands, the football player with dyed blood-red hair who spent most of his time riling up his teammate who was constantly rolling his eyes with an exasperated expression, and friendliest person in the whole school joined to his hip, Malachi found himself being stared at like the rare animal at the zoo.

His mismatched grey and black eyes didn't help much but he had grown his hair to the point where he could shield his eyes from their curious gazes. The walking circus that followed him however, was thoroughly amusing for most of the student population. Wherever they went their tired eyes followed, and Malachi couldn't blame them. With their finals just around the corner every random bout of laughter was healing.

Malachi was having a hard time studying already, he couldn't handle the spike in the last-minute workload and he wanted to politely ask the circus to *fuck off*, but something in their eyes told him that there was no way that was going to hinder them whatsoever.

He couldn't even ignore them and busy himself with his phone.

Sure, there were other people in the school that Malachi spoke to, but that didn't mean that he was going to go out of his way to find them and talk to them.

Thankfully, when he was left alone — which on its own was a rare occurrence — when he escaped from the circus, was when their friends decided to drop by, which Malachi was thankful for.

He didn't want to weigh them down.

Another thing Malachi had realised over the last few days was that his school was really small.

Not the campus, the student body population.

Malachi soon learnt that the circus attached to him ran in the same social circles — which were slowly trying to suck him in and because of the project, he was practically forced to interact with them.

They were all interesting in their own right and Malachi found himself clicking pictures of the interactions.

He couldn't understand why but he couldn't bring himself to delete them.

flashback

It's burning with a fire.
Taking me higher,
Riding a storm, breaking every norm.
I'm starting to side-track.
Stuck in a flashback.

Time is walking away, I'm running astray.
Lost in a story at the back of my head.
This time there is no thread,
Running through the haze in the maze
It seems as though all there is to feel is dread,

Every wrong turn is taking me to the monster,
But I'm strong, I'm a fighter.
Don't wait for me.
I'll be back.
No longer stuck in a flashback.

~ ✦ ~

simply holding on to *what if*

To the stars,

Human beings make mistakes. That's what we are told from a very young age, but what if it is a huge conspiracy and the reality is that human beings cannot make mistakes, and there is a large population of humans who are just lazy and their laziness is the reason for this reality?

Maybe, people were just so tired of the idea of striving to be perfect that most of them decided that enough was enough, and they can't do this anymore, and perfection is merely an illusion.

Maybe that's why we fell.

Could it be that a child's imagination is the fuel to their powers and since these dreams are crushed at a young age this reduces their power of imagination, and everything that they think of appears to have the shadow of reality lurking behind it?

This shadow can actually become the reason we are held back adding more to the fact that humans gave up. Every video you see in school tells you about trying to do your best, but it never tells us to be the best. This is justified by saving a child from the stress and fear of failure which are later on the same words that have no meaning to the life of an adult, because these are just fancy words that they have no time for.

If all the inhabitants of a planet can make this mistake, my mistake does not have that much of a value and can even become a cloak for all the mistakes that are to be made by humans in the future.

~Liberosis, Remington.

~ ✦ ~

The night danced against the flow of time.

She swayed to the drum of her own beat.

They often fought, but continued the same dance day after day.

At the corner of his bed sat a bag in which lay a new phone. Someone must have noticed the lack of it. Having finished most of his work he had nothing to do and sleep did not want to embrace him. Malachi had activated it about two hours ago and had been dreading the number of unread messages.

Malachi was alone albeit his house was buzzing, which was odd to say the least, but Malachi couldn't bring himself to care.

He was all alone.

His phone was having a seizure but he couldn't bring himself to care. Malachi had always been on his own even though he was surrounded by people. No one really saw him but there was a light flickering within, this flame turned into a furnace when he was with the people he was comfortable with. They were still *there*; he just couldn't see them clearly through his tear-filled eyes.

He looked fragile, but he had the strength of an army.

Malachi was thrown into a universe in which he did not belong. In this universe he had found a few celestials for whom he was grateful, even though he didn't show it. He had a space station within which

Acenath, a Lonely Astronaut, is trying to find her way back to her world. He had the North Star who was calling out to him and steering him back on course. Devon had been their knight in shining armour but now the armour was dented and the knight was scarred with the memories of forgotten battles. He was their voice of reason. Their Moral Compass. He had recently met the Quasar whose smile fought the overwhelming darkness all while embracing the shadows, and a Meteorite who burned with an alluring flame. Occasionally, Malachi could see the soft dance of the Aurora Borealis light years away.

In Malachi's universe there was no light, even with the celestials that surrounded him, there was only darkness. Comforting and accepting, beautiful in its own way, it brings out the best in everyone. In Malachi's mind this was Remington.

But now darkness was swallowing him whole.

Remington was the stars; but now that he was gone, Malachi was blind all over again.

The light was gone.

The Lonely Astronaut was calling out to him but her screams were a mere whisper in his murky mind and the North Star was hidden — almost fading away, but he was trying his best to fight it.

Malachi was not leaning into the darkness.

He was the darkness.

Malachi begrudgingly picked up his phone. He glanced through the various messages, didn't have the energy to reply any of them, but made a mental note to get back to them. Malachi probably wouldn't reply to his messages, however his emails had a special place in his heart. Upon opening his inbox, he saw two mails from the same email

ID. He did not recognize it. Malachi opened them to deem their importance.

His eyes ran over the first email thrice.
He couldn't believe the words he was reading.

Sae-Hee Ryong <ryongsaehee@gmail.com>
7:56 AM

To me.

Dear Malachi Elakrab,

I'm positive you don't know how I am and the chances of you opening this email are really not in my favour however in the words of Eros *'I will leave this to the stars.'* I know or at least I like to tell myself that I knew Eros Remington. I befriended him at university. I met him while he played the piano, yet another one of his various talents. He was one of a kind and will always be. I'm not writing this email to you as one of condolence. I'm writing to let you know that I sent out the letters.

The ones addressed to you that he never sent. Eros forgot them back in the dorm when he was headed home so I mailed them for him.

I played the piano (well I tried to) when I heard about his accident. I heard you didn't get to meet him when he returned—no one did. I still don't understand why he took the earlier flight. I wish I had stopped him, but he melted my resolve. He just had to surprise all of you. I don't even know why I am writing this to you. An absolute stranger. But the way he spoke about you made me feel as though I knew everything about you and all of your friends.

The idea of writing a letter is beautiful but I'm happy with the technological advancements.

~Ryong Sae-Hee

Malachi stared at the screen for a few seconds.

'This must be the insomniac.' He thought and opened the second email.

~ ✦ ~

Sae-Hee Ryong <ryongsaehee@gmail.com>
8:30 AM

To me.

Dear Malachi Elakrab,

It is still me.

I can tell why Eros was in love with you.
He did not fail to mention that. He also told me that you are apprehensive of new people so I would like to introduce myself to you through this email, because Eros has rubbed off on me.

I'm a criminology student and I want to get into law. My drug of choice is caffeine and talking about myself seems a lot like a university application. Exceedingly formal and unnecessary.

My Snapchat is ryongsaebell (like rung the bell but with parts of my name) yeah, I want to punch my 13-year-old self for choosing that. So, if emails seem too slow in order to talk to me, if you choose to, you can use Snapchat.

You know everyone in his dorm wanted to punch him at one point or another. Simply because he always spoke about you but never spoke to you. We used to call you… well, we still do refer to you as the light of his life.

You are the light of his life, and we, the rest of us, are everything that follows. But that's just shadows but in that darkness emerges a beautiful force to be reckoned with — man he really rubbed off on me.

~Ryong Sae-Hee

~ ✦ ~

Malachi couldn't understand this email. His brain shut down after the first three lines of the email.

I can tell why Eros was in love with you.

What could she have possibly meant by that?

Malachi's imagination ran amok.

'maybe this letter was a joke?'
OBVIOUSLY, WHO COULD EVER LOVE YOU?
'maybe the letter was a mistake?'
LOVING YOU WAS THE BIGGEST MISTAKE HE COULD HAVE EVER MADE.
'maybe the letter was true?'
THEN THE ONLY PERSON WHO LOVED YOU IS DEAD.
'breathe.'
DO THE WORLD A FAVOUR AND STOP BREATHING.
'breathe.'
'come on.'
'breathe.'

'breathe.'

Malachi couldn't concentrate.

He was drowning and the walls had fallen apart.

~ ✦ ~

tragedy in the making

to the stars,

i don't understand the entire concept of chasing happiness.

i can't.

i don't want to.

i don't want to live knowing that i've been chasing something that kept on running away from me.

it hurts, please make it stop.

~idyllically, Malachi.

~ ✦ ~

Mornings in the Elakrab house had no value, simply put the residents who'd barely slept in the first place, to appreciate the morning that announced the birth of a new day.

With one last glance at his room Malachi made his way to the dining room. His bag felt heavier than usual. The letters with their heavy, unknown contents lay there untouched. He couldn't find it in himself to leave them in his room. He couldn't abandon them.

The house felt cold and the air felt heavy, in fact, there was nothing homely about Malachi's house. The only thing it did was make him miss his previous home. Now that was a home. Where people lived and loved.

The current house was a palace of mannequins and a rest stop for people with faces of someone you once knew. Unlike most people in his neighbourhood, Malachi's parents earned their name and their wealth. The people that lived in Malachi's house went on with their own lives and didn't hinder each other's movements, but nothing was constant.

Actually, there was something constant in the Elakrab household but only one resident was aware of it.

The pain; Malachi had a pain in his chest and he couldn't remember a time when it hadn't been there.

~ ✦ ~

After inhaling his cup of coffee Malachi made his way to the car, he didn't want to sit in it and quite frankly he'd rather walk.

To the rest of the world Malachi doesn't walk.
He glides, almost like he had no ties to Earth and gravity didn't work on him.

In their eyes he glides like a dancer.
But Malachi glides like a puppet, adhering to his ruthless puppeteer's every will, his anxiety.

~ ✦ ~

Even with the songs blaring in through his earphones, they couldn't drown out the voices in his head.

There were moments when the songs would drown out the voices but this time, they were really failing him. He was so lost in his mind that he didn't even notice that three songs had just flown by. He was so lost in his mind that he didn't notice that the car was stuck in traffic. He concluded that his head was hurting so bad that he thought the world around him had frozen. The distant honking of the cars and yelling of the people around him grounded him but the words from Ryong Sae-

Hee's email were ringing in the back of his head.

I can tell why Eros was in love with you.

He wanted to erase them from his mind, but they gave him a weird sense of comfort and fed a new chorus led by regret and fear in his head.

As his car began moving again, he wondered if Eros' letters answered any of his questions.

He had been contemplating but now that he was alone in his car with the silence suffocating him, he reached into his bag which he had been hugging to his chest and opened the letter which had been marked by an unassuming star on the envelope itself.

To the stars,

I learnt about love recently, there are various types of love.
Aside from the romantic love that people are always chasing and dreaming.
I also learned about the other types of love that aren't romantic.
The love you feel for your friends.
The love you feel for your family.
The love you feel for fictional characters.

It comes in different shapes and forms but we chase after the fairytale love portrayed by glorified love stories.

There are many times when love is unrequited.
When people aren't equally in love.
When people grow apart and feel their love weaken.
After learning of these things, I have come to a conclusion.
The romantic love that everyone chases after is not meant for everyone… I didn't think it was meant for me.
The unconditional love.
The fairytale love: Is the same love I feel for you.
But terms and conditions apply, this love doesn't exist for me.

I believe it's unrequited.

Malachi Elakrab, I have never been this sure about anything.
I am in love with you. And this is:
Not the love you feel for your friends.
Not the love you feel for your family.
Not an infatuation.

But the romantic love. It's always been there; I was just made aware of it.

Funny, isn't it?
Even with Cupid's name I can't attain love.
I have found it but at some point, I thought I'd be happier not knowing… however, I stand corrected.

Eros Remington, the boy who found love.
That's it.
How anticlimactic.

~Loving you, Eros.

~ ◆ ~

Malachi froze. He read and re-read the lines repeatedly but the words didn't change. He was sitting frozen on his seat with his heart beating a million beats per second.

He couldn't process the words and his eyes were burning. He didn't even realise that he was crying until a tear fell on the letter. The paper was discoloured to begin with but the tear burned into the paper.

'How could you have been in love with me?' His voice barely rose to a whisper.

~ ◆ ~

Malachi barely managed to pull himself together when the car stopped in front of his school. He could barely find the strength to open his door. His hands were weak and shaky, almost like they had been further weakened by the weight of the letter. He struggled with the door and his legs struggled to support his body.

He looked around to see people walking around him. Everyone looked like they were at peace with their minds even while fighting their own demons; while Malachi felt like he was losing yet another battle.

He often felt inferior and pale in comparison to the rest of the students but this time he felt envious. He looked around to see if Jay had shown up but he found himself to be all alone.

How did he always end up here?

Alone.

~ ◆ ~

are we okay?
definitely *okay*, because i think
we are far from it

To the stars,

The entire concept of existing is rather strange and painful on its own, right from the process of one's birth to one's death. Directly or indirectly someone is in pain. To make this entire ordeal of life even more miserable we have to undergo the strange and ever-so-confusing period of adolescence. Where we are all told that we are all in the same boat and told that -This is just a phase - I like to believe that we are all in the same boat and in the same ocean, but in different realities.

~Liberosis, Remington.

~ ✦ ~

Thankfully, the lectures flew by.

But it wasn't only the lectures that flew by... it was the world as well.

The Quasar.
The Lonely Astronaut.
The Meteorite.
The North Star.

Everyone was jovial and loud which made Malachi feel more out of place than usual, and tired if anything.

'Can we go to the Willow tree?' The question was entirely directed to the Lonely Astronaut and the North Star.

'I don't like it here,' he whispered again.

The Meteorite and the Quasar looked at the trio in front of them. They could understand the gist of the exchange happening in front of them and since they were obviously not being invited... they might as well invite themselves.

'Where are we going?'
'We? You weren't invited!'

'We have to work on our project, does that ring a bell?' The Lonely Astronaut's face fell almost instantly.
The North Star was just relieved that he hadn't taken this class — for one, he did not even know the name of the subject to begin with.

The Meteorite and the Lonely Astronaut began bickering.

'We can do this project later,' she argued.
'It's for Devon's safety,' he pointed out like it was the most obvious thing in the whole world, 'after all he is going to be left with you.'

'And?' Her icy tone accompanied by the look on her face was enough for him to cough up the truth.

'I'm bored and I don't have practice today,' his shoulders sagged dramatically while he began to put his stuff away and follow Malachi and the Quasar who were slowly backing away, 'and I want to see what you guys are going to do.'

'Curiosity killed the cat.'
'A cat has nine lives.'
'Yeah, well you are on your last one.'
'In that case, satisfaction brought it back.'
'You are insufferable.'
'You are impossible.'
'That fact that I exist makes me possible.'
'You are- '

'Please shut up,' The North Star cut in.

The Lonely Astronaut flipped off the North Star and began walking beside Quasar who was struggling to make small talk with the obsidian-haired boy who looked right through her, while the North Star rolled his eyes at the Meteorite.

They couldn't hear the music which obviously meant that the twins weren't there.

It seemed as though the beautiful lights had been dimmed. The sunlight had lost its rhythm, it no longer had a tune to dance to and no one was waiting by the fountain to hear the music.

It felt mundane.

'Malachi? You okay?' the concerned Quasar's voice brought him back to the present. She was waving her white cardigan-covered arm in front of him.

It was in that very moment that he had realised that he had stopped walking.

He was frozen.

His eyes were trained to the piano, he looked at the Lonely Astronaut — almost as if he was asking for permission.
'Yeah,' he whispered, 'I'm sorry.'

The Quasar blinked twice at his lost and empty response; even though she had grown accustomed to his behaviour, this had taken her by surprise.

Malachi walked over to the piano and sat down.

'You can play?' The Meteorite asked with mirth in his voice.
'Stupid question.' The Lonely Astronaut shook her head with her eyes trained at her cousin.

Malachi's fingers danced over the keys.
His long fingers were seemingly made for this.

They were hesitant.
They were lingering.

And suddenly, he was no longer the only person playing the piano.

Kamaria.

'You've been talking to many people.'
'Yeah,' Malachi nodded, 'it's tiring.'

'The letters hurt you, didn't they?' She didn't even bother to beat around the bush like she usually did.

'They didn't,' he said with a newfound confidence, 'I did.'
'You know, you can't take all the blame.'
'Well, I can't exactly blame him now, can I?'

'Always the pessimist.'
'I'm actually a realist.' He paused before muttering under his breath. "Unless you know to bring back the dead."
'Well then your world must suck.' She ignored his last statement.

Malachi scoffed at her childish response.

'I'll see you soon.' With that she was gone.

The group around him were all seated on the grass — they all looked relaxed and at ease.

I promise the stars, I won't let the world pass me by.

Malachi's mind flashed back to the first time he broke his promise to the stars and he ended up meeting Jay.

Malachi was merely seven years old when he had promised the stars that he would bake Remington's birthday cake on his own. But he didn't. He couldn't. He was dragged to one of his parent's parties. Where he hung around with Acenath and Devon who sat with their brooding friend, sympathising.

They felt helpless.

The following day at Eros' birthday party there was a cake brought in by one of his friends. A petite looking girl with long blonde hair and bright green eyes. She looked like a doll and Remington *hugged* her to express his joy and gratitude.

A hug that was rightly Malachi's.

Malachi watched the exchange from afar with a sour expression on his face when a soft bout of laughter alerted him. Next to him, Malachi saw a boy around his age dressed in a dark green jumper and black jeans. His hair was black as the night and his eyes matched his jumper. He gave Malachi a Cheshire smile and rocked on his green wheelie shoes.

'Hi Malachi, I'm Jay.'

'How do you know my name?' he asked innocently. 'Because.' The newcomer shrugged and his response caused Malachi to blink twice. 'My name is Jay. I'm your jealousy,' with that he extended his hand to an impressed Malachi.

'Oh,' he all but managed.

Malachi had no idea what he was talking about but he was in awe of the boy's diction and sophisticated manners.

'I can hear your thoughts, so you should just be honest with me,' he smiled cheekily, 'And thank you for the compliment.'

Malachi blushed at the realization but tried to brush it off.

'That's so cool!' he cheered, 'Do you want to meet my friends and read their thoughts?' 'Actually, I can only read your thoughts,' he explained, 'only you can see me and talk to me.' 'Wait—so you are only mine?' he asked with stars in his eyes. 'Yup,' he popped the 'p' while rocking on his heels.

I wish Eros was only mine.

'That's why I am here.' 'What?' Malachi tilted his head in confusion. 'I can read your thoughts remember? I'm here because you are jealous.'

'Oh.'

'So, when I'll stop feeling like this what will happen to you?'
'I'll also go away.'
'I don't want you to go away.'
'It's okay. I'll be back,' he shrugged off the concern.

'What do your friends call you?'

'My name… Malachi, remember?'
'No,' Jay laughed, 'like a nickname.'
'Like a nickname?' Malachi parroted.
'Yeah.'
Malachi thought about it for a second before asking, 'Why do you want to know?'

'Because.'

'Because, why?'
'Because — I have a nickname for you.'
'Really?' Malachi was coloured surprised.
'Lily,' Jay supplied with a cheeky smile.

'Huh?'

Malachi couldn't get the logic.
'Your name has 'L' and I' in it,' Jay explained.
'So?' Malachi still couldn't get the logic.
'When you say Li — forget it,' Jay muttered, 'you remind me of a Lily.'

'Why?'

'Malachi! We are cutting the cake,' Devon called out and grabbed his hand and pulled him to where the cake was being cut. Remington was not near the cake. In fact, he was with Acenath who was also looking for Malachi.

Malachi was confused.

They ran over and Remington pulled Malachi away from Devon and handed him the knife. Malachi, looked at him funny — he then held Malachi's hand which had the knife. Devon and Acenath joined in and the four cut the cake.

From the corner of his eyes Malachi could see Jay wave goodbye and then he
was gone.

And in the following week, Malachi asked everyone around him what they
knew about Lilies.

~ ✦ ~

Malachi felt at ease and so did his audience.

Later on that day, he found himself with the theater club.
The Quasar claimed that the visit would be worth it and she was
probably right.

The theatre club was in the middle of auditions.
Malachi and the Quasar sat down a few seats behind the teacher who
was holding the auditions. They didn't even know what the play was
about, nor did they know which parts the members of the theatre club
were auditioning for.

They were just there.

The twins were playing instruments for the auditions — which explained
why the lawn was lifeless — making the domed auditorium come to
life.

The lights they emitted were strong.

Aurora Borealis.
Nature's Symphony.

All the auditions were good but nothing particularly stood out, and
soon, audition after audition flew by, and then they were done.

The Quasar was wrong.

The duo swiftly made their way to the exit.
Malachi yet again found himself in the cold, pale glass hallways.

~ ✦ ~

race against time

To the stars,

they say follow the lights home... but you are my home.

~idyllically, Malachi.

The day flew by — quicker than usual.

Well, mostly because Malachi was lost in his mind and could not process the concept of time. But the second Malachi found himself in the math lecture, he felt like he was pulling himself out of quicksand. It seemed hopeless, painful, unnecessary, and awfully time-consuming. His head was beginning to ache and his book no longer had numbers, only alphabets. The rest of his class was in the same state. Everyone's face had a bright red question mark painted on it.

The Meteorite sat next to him; he was seemingly functioning on his own tangent. He was a few sums ahead of the class and had a very bored expression on his face. Malachi had no idea what made the Meteorite sit next to him but he had a strong feeling it had something to do with the Lonely Astronaut.

Something about the Meteorite set off all Malachi's in-built alarms.

'I didn't know you could play the piano,' he stated, leaning back in his chair.
'Most people don't,' Malachi murmured.

'*Most people* don't know anything about you.'

Does he want to befriend me?

'Acenath told me you play football.'

Why?

'Barely,' he whispered and went back to his work.
'You should come by during practice,' the Meteorite acted like he didn't hear Malachi's response.

'I'm really bad,' Malachi declared a little louder this time.

I don't want people to see me play.

'That, or you don't want others to see you play?' he scoffed.

The Meteorite could read his mind.

'Don't let your fears control you,' The Meteorite muttered in disdain, looking straight ahead at the board.

The rest of the class went on in the same fashion. The Meteorite would ask Malachi a question and Malachi would answer. At this point he didn't even know why he was answering.

'How did you and Acenath become friends?' Malachi finally asked.

'We aren't exactly friends.'

'Then why are you always with her?' Malachi's tone came off as intrusive, but this was more interesting than the sums that he had given up on.

'We got paired together for Mr Salone's project,' he paused in thought, 'and she's friends with Rosie and René.'

Malachi nodded.

'We wanted to make sure that she was staying clean cause of your friend's accident,' he added sharply, while running his hands through his hair.

Malachi froze and the Meteorite continued.

'Did you seriously think that you were the only one affected by his death?' He clicked his tongue, 'The rest of the world still exists and your friends are so focused on keeping you afloat that they keep on forgetting about themselves.' He turned his sharp gaze to Malachi. 'I don't know you and honestly I don't care about you, but the people who I do care about — their happiness lies in the balance with you. So, I really don't care what you do, but if you hurt them — and I don't care if you are in pain — grow the fuck up and learn to deal with your own damned problems.'

The Meteorite was a swinging pendulum.
The Meteorite burned away fear and immortalised himself in your memory.

Malachi didn't answer.
He wanted to thank him for filling him in on the Lonely Astronaut's situation, but he couldn't bring himself to say another word.

They fell into silence.
A comfortable silence.
A comfortable silence in a chaotic math class, and the only reason it was comfortable was the fact that Malachi was lost in his head while struggling to hold back his tears.

As soon as the lecture got over, Malachi swiftly bid Vince farewell.

He had practice with the other meteorites and Malachi had to get away from him.

Malachi could see the Quasar getting out of another interrogation room and she was *obviously* not alone. There were planets hovering around her. They all had carefree smiles and heavy bags in their hands and under their eyes, but they seemed relieved to leave whichever interrogation room they were getting out of. Malachi understood why they felt like that. From the same interrogation hall stumbled out two suspects — they however, were scowling.

Cordelia Delta Blue and Arthur Williams.

They didn't seem in the brightest of moods; the swim team's captain and not-so-secret weapon was arguing with the student body president who was cleaning his reading glasses. Malachi got along very well with Arthur Williams; he was one of the few sane people in the glass prison. He was absolutely brilliant and seamlessly got along with everyone, and quite frankly, there wasn't a single person who didn't like him, teachers included.

Malachi had not seen him in quite some time, probably because he was busy doing experiments and rejecting universities while Malachi was locked in his room trapped with his mind.

As Malachi walked towards the Quasar who was tying up her long blonde locks, Arthur stopped him.

A Supernova.

Powerful.
Miraculous.
Rare.
Ethereal.

'Malachi!' he called with an infectious smile, 'I haven't seen you in forever.'
'Hey, yeah — I've been busy,' Malachi couldn't look him in the eye — he felt guilty.
'That's totally cool, just let me know if you need anything.' Something in his emerald-like eyes made Malachi want to bury himself in guilt.

'Arthur!' Cordelia all but screeched, 'you can't just walk away while we were talking.'
'I'm sorry, but that was not a conversation — that was your monologue.'
'Arthur!' she whined, 'this is serious.'
'It's really not.'
'It is.'
'The perception of the seriousness of the situation is subjective — hence neither one of us is right nor wrong,' he teased her with a mischievous glint in his eyes.

Malachi felt a shiver run down his spine when he saw Cordelia's brilliant blue eye twitch.

'Cordelia! I need a favour.'
'Would you wait, you impatient imbecile? Can't you see that- Oh! Talon, I'm sorry,' she smiled sheepishly, 'what do you need?'
Malachi and the Supernova exchanged a look.
'It's for Mr Salone's, class we just- '

Malachi tuned out yet again when a sharp ringing sound pierced his ear, causing him to wince, but no one noticed.

'Oh yeah! Sure, I've got practice in five any which way and you guys can totally come with me,' the girl with the bright blue eyes exclaimed.

'See, Arthur!' she whined again, 'they have already started with their project; we haven't even picked a topic.'

So, that's the conflict.

'Even Acenath and Vince have started; I refuse to finish after the bloodhound.'
'Your personal vendetta is not going to be the reason we rush through our project.'

The Supernova was logical and the swim team's captain was emotional, and to no one's surprise and Malachi's horror, this duo got along a little too well with the Lonely Astronaut and the North Star.

'We can work after you are done with practice; I'll be in the Physics lab.'
'Um-no! Arthur you said that last week and disappeared for the rest of the day. You are coming with me.'
'*Ex Nihilo Nihil Fit*, but at least there will be people there as witnesses just in case you decide to murder me.'

She made a face at him and stormed off with the rest of them following her.

The path to the swimming pool was short and simple but keeping up with Cordelia was in no way an easy task. She took large strides with her long legs, promptly storming past our world – she was storming towards her world.

The water.

Water and light weaved a blanket together, they lived harmoniously and seemingly brought to life the gym's otherwise plain ceiling – glistening and glittering.

The story in the water on its own was very different. It was the home of the humans with the heart of mermaids and mermen, their bodies moving in the water gracefully, showing no resistance. As they swam, the water splashed ever so strongly, but the sound wasn't harsh – it was almost synchronised. The mermaids and mermen were falling, their hearts were falling from their home to the mortal world.

Comets.

Malachi hadn't even registered the fact that the freckled swim team's captain had already changed and was getting ready to dive in. Malachi fumbled for his camera and got ready to click a picture.

He felt like something was going to happen.

The comets were moving.
Rhythmically.
Gracefully.
Peacefully.

Everyone was in awe of them. Well... they didn't have much of an audience.

All they had was coaches who were just living another day in their mundane lives.

The Supernova was peacefully observing the comets while making swimming puns every now and then. The Quasar was humouring him but her attention was really on the swimmers, and Malachi watched the comets in unadulterated awe, and the sight before him was enough to keep his mind off of Vince's words.

'*Water* they doing?'
'Swimming,' Malachi deadpanned.

'This day has gone by just swimmingly.'
'I'm going to shove you into the deep end,' The Quasar quipped.
'That'll just be more proof that I really have gone off the deep end.'

Malachi was grateful that he had learned to tune people out.

'She's going to do it.'

Malachi was taken aback by the change of tone.

Who was going to do what?

And there she was. Cordelia Delta Blue was in her true element. She was doing the butterfly and her toned muscles were gleaming in the water as she splashed.

Malachi ran to the front of the pool.

She was getting closer and the second before the camera flashed she had leaped to the highest and done a half-somersault and her body twisted mid-air, and in a blink of an eye, she was back in the water swimming to the other side.

Malachi snapped the picture of the shooting star mid-air in between both her worlds. The world where her heart belongs and the world where her body is trapped.

Malachi and the Quasar waited for her while the Supernova was thoroughly amused by their reaction.

'Cordelia? They need to leave, can you finish their interview?'
She ignored him — *maybe she didn't hear him?*

'Delia? You are wasting their time.'

She swam away.

'Cordelia Delta Blue, I will leave if you don't get out and do the interview.'

The comet froze.

'You wouldn't.'

'Try me.'

'I don't believe you,' she challenged.

'If I start with my work you should know better than anyone that you can't get me back until I'm done.'

She glared daggers at him and started to get out of the pool. 'I'm taking a break,' she called out to no one in particular.

Malachi got ready to record, standing steady while his hair began tickling the hollow of his eyes. Although, it was a constant bother that he had learnt to live with.

'Hey, I'm Cordelia Delta Blue and the water is my home. Being in the water in general gives me a sense of belonging,' she smiled wistfully, 'funny, as it started off as an obligation. I used to cry when I had to swim and now, I don't want to get out of the water.'

To make her point she gracefully dived back into the water, Malachi moved the camera to follow her and she continued speaking.

'In the water, I'm myself and I'm not obligated to adhere to people — it helped me figure out what I want to do in the future. The water made me free and it is my home. So, I want to make all those who stay in the water free and safe. Without the water I am nothing.' With that she swam away, as if nothing had happened and Malachi stopped recording.

Okay, then.

'Yeah... that's Cordelia.'

She was a force to be reckoned with.

A Comet.

The Halley's Comet.

The Quasar bid Malachi and the Supernova goodbye and the duo made their way to the lab after informing the fuming Halley's Comet.

~ ✦ ~

The lab seemed cold and clinical. It was well-maintained but seemed abandoned, and despite the bright white lights, it was dark.

The Supernova seemed to know his way around the lab, and began gathering equipment to start one of his experiments Malachi could only assume.

Malachi had no idea how one brain could be this sharp.

'Malachi? Can you please help me with this?' he called out while gesturing to a wooden contraption, his movement caused the small tattoo of a sunflower on his wrist to peek out from under his deep green sweater. Malachi complied.

'So, why did you really disappear?' *This was the glint.*
Malachi froze.
He couldn't exactly make a run for it now.

'Um...I...'
'You have to talk to someone about it and by the looks of if you haven't even mentioned this to one person, have you?'
'Well people are *aware*.'
'People are also aware of gravity.'
'Arthur — it's just complicated.'
'Then simplify it.'

If it were only that simple.

Malachi opened his mouth to say something but four individuals stumbled in through the door.

Their laughter sounded light, strong and free.

They had a wall up around them, maybe to protect themselves or maybe because only a few deemed worthy to get close to them.

They had infectious smiles and seemed at ease with each other even though they were worlds apart. Yet something just clicked with them and since then they were stuck.

René Anders, a force to reckon with.
Her heart of gold that never really closes its doors on anyone.
Her passion and love burns like an eternal flame.

Sebastian Smalls, he stood strong and reliable.
He stands by you through thick and thin.
He brings comfort and hope with him.
He's like the Earth; his embrace feels like home.

Parker Darrow, the embodiment of reserved and composed.
He was adaptable and serene.
He's an unpredictable and uncontrollable force of nature which takes everyone by storm.
He's fluid and calming, like the deep and unknown waters.
You don't know what lies within and yet you can't help but be drawn.

Marco Rosenetti, as dual as day and night.
No one really knows what goes on in his mind.
He can be as gentle as a whisper if you survive the unforgiving hurricane.
As versatile as air.

The eccentric, electric elements.

No one really knows how the group came into existence but one day they were just there. They help each other and weirdly complement each other. In a school where everyone was disintegrating, their fragments made a stronger whole and there they stood.

They hadn't seemed to notice the duo in the lab. They were in their own world, the corners of their eyes crinkling and gleaming smiles adorned their faces. Malachi had often seen them with Vince but they had their other friends as well. They smiled brightly at each other.

Malachi wondered what went through their minds.

Maybe they were trying to make up for the year they'd spent as acquaintances?

Maybe they were afraid of how quickly time was moving and how these days were soon going to be gone?

Malachi spoke to them in passing like most people, but there was something enticing about them.

They came to a halt when their eyes landed on the duo, but their smiles were still glued on.

They waved at the duo and moved their conversation to soft whispers which often escalated to loud comments that simmered down again with laughter.
They were in their own world. They all had their laptops open and were typing away.

No one understood what they spoke about but there were never moments of awkward silence often seen in a new group of friends. It was almost like they had known each other their whole lives and this was just a reunion.

They seemed to help each other and made up for each other's shortcomings. They created the perfect balance even while creating absolute chaos.

Malachi couldn't help but admire them.

The Ethereal Elements.

The Supernova was almost done setting up his apparatus when he looked at Malachi with concern in his eyes.

'What happened?' he whispered.
'It doesn't matter. What are you doing?'
'You and I both know you have no interest in physics so use a more believable diversion to change the topic.'

'Arthur - I - it's not that important.'

'Malachi...' he trailed off, 'you disappeared; how can it not be important?'

'They care about you Malachi.' Kamaria words rang in his mind.
'As you know, Remington passed away.'

Silence.

'Turns out he — he came early to surprise *me*,' he choked, his voice shaking, 'and he got into an accident on his way home from the airport.'

Silence prevailed.

'He sent out letters and he said that *loved* me,' His voice was still shaking, 'and he died because he lov-loved me.'

'Malachi, he didn't die because he loves you,' the Supernova paused, 'love never killed anyone.'
'Wars were fought for the sake of love.'
'Wars were fought because of the egos of men.'
'Romeo and Juliet.'
'The exception, not the law.'
'Cleopatra and Mark Antony.'
'Political mayhem,' the Supernova quickly countered.

'Love isn't the cause of death or pain,' Fire called out while adjusting her hairband, 'love poisoned by people and mobilised into a weapon is the cause.'

'Ignore love's advocate here,' Water.
'Her point of view is entirely biased,' Air.
'Who needs love? It's the biggest and longest running scam,' Earth.

'My view may be biased but yours is tainted.'
'Aha! So, you confess your point of view is biased.'
'At least it's not tainted.'
'Fancy word for the same thing.'
'I — how is *tainted* a fancy word?'

Tainted love causes pain and creates a biased opinion.

Fire and Air.
René and Marco.

The perpetually bickering duo. They've known each other for a little under six years and in their opinion, six years too much. Fire needs Air to live and they thrive off each other. The perfect balance *can* exist. Albeit it turns out to be a rather tall order.

Water and Earth snickered at their friends. The bickering was an everyday occurrence that never failed to be amusing. As the bickering grew softer and childish the sound of clacking keys became louder and consistent.

'He didn't die because he *loved* me,' Malachi gravely swallowed, 'he died because he loved *me*.'

The clacking of the keys ceased.

'Malachi, you made no contribution to that.'

'No! I convinced him to apply, I - I -.'
'You did nothing wrong,' the Supernova hissed, 'what happened was not your fault and it never will be.'

Malachi's eyes started watering and before he knew it he was running out of the lab; through his glassy eyes he could see the students walk in and out of interrogation rooms. Their expressions steely or full of emotion.

Everyone was crumbling.
Disintegrating.
Collapsing.

But they hid it well, they were still alive.
The day had been a success.

It was no longer about learning and coming into your own person.
It was about staying alive and fitting into someone else's definition of perfection.

Merely fitting into a mould.

Tearing yourself apart to fit into a mould.

Malachi's chest began to hurt.
The numbing pain was significantly stronger.

In that moment he did what he did best.
He ran.
He ignored the Supernova's voice.

He threw himself into his car and then he was off. His eyes were glued to the window. The sky was a beautiful shade of purple. The busy city lights were blending well into the canvas.

He was still black and white in a kaleidoscopic world of colours.

stationary fragments of a broken mind

~ ✦ ~

To the stars,

i don't know how to say goodbye.

~idyllically, Malachi.

Maybe the pain wasn't as bad as he felt.
Maybe this was all an illusion — manifested by his nightmares that now blurred into reality.

For the first time in a long time Sleep was stomping on his eyelids, beckoning him to escape his reality — but Malachi fought her and pushed her away. He didn't want to transition from one nightmare to the other without putting up a fight, but the car's cold atmosphere amplified Sleep's merciless assault and Malachi felt as though every fibre of his being was surrendering.

The slow-moving traffic wasn't helping him and he couldn't help but feel like the world had turned against him.

'Did you seriously think that you were the only one affected by his death?' Vince's words rang through his mind.

'The rest of the world still exists and your friends are so focused on keeping you afloat that they keep on forgetting about themselves.'

If they were fighting to keep him afloat; why couldn't he?

'Grow the fuck up and learn to deal with your own damned problems.'

Grow up? Growing pain refers to the pain we feel in our adolescence due to the actual growth of our physical being — but what if that pain also refers to the heartache we feel while we grow up and grow apart? What if the pain is our farewell to a reality that faded into a memory?

~ ◆ ~

Malachi struggled to open his door. He scrambled out of the car and stumbled down the front yard.

He was exhausted. He wanted to scream at the skies but he didn't have the energy to. His legs seemed to have a mind of their own and they led him to who knows where. Malachi's soft footsteps broke the ever-present silence in the house of mannequins. On his way to his unknown destination, he passed the living room where the North Star and the Lonely Astronaut lay dead asleep.

They were probably waiting for me.

Realization flashed in his tried eyes.
Tomorrow was the *day*. The *four* of them would always stay over the night before and fool around the whole weekend, but it hadn't happened last month because of the *accident*.

Malachi made his way to the piano in the next room and as much as he wanted to throw himself onto the soft bean-bags in the library he had no control over his body.

He played *the* melancholic tune and let his emotions escape into the ivory keys as his fingers danced alone.

'I told you they love you,' a honeyed whisper sounded.
'And I told you it'll be their demise.'
'Malachi, look at the bags under their eyes,' she sounded smug, 'this is probably the first time they've slept in the last week.' *Because of you.*

'I had the honour of knowing you Malachi — but I don't know who you are anymore. You are using Eros as an excuse at this point,' her tattooed hand grabbed his. 'Malachi this is an amalgamation of all the pain you have ever felt.'

The music got louder.

'It's not,' came his broken whisper.
'Malachi, why are you lying to me?'

Malachi held a note and his shoulders sagged.

'I'm not,' he repeated himself.
'Then why are you lying to yourself?'
'I'm not.'

'Don't lie to me Malachi,' she laughed, 'I won't understand your pain but I do understand that he was your whole universe.'
'He is.'
'*People* make our universe Malachi,' she smiled sadly, 'don't forget the others.'

The music got faster.

'Fine Malachi, I'll humour you. What are you doing?'
'I'm coping.'
'Find a healthier coping mechanism.'
'Mine is better that Acenath's,' he hissed coldly.

The music became slower the second she got up.

'I know,' he heaved a sigh, 'that was uncalled for.'
'Then why'd you say it Malachi?'

'You know you can't hurt me, right? You still think hurting them now will save them from a greater pain in the future, don't you?'
'It's worth the shot,' he shrugged.
'You know you can't do the same to me right?'
'I can try.'
'Then that will be your demise.'

'Mocking me, are we?'
'Not fun to be on the other side, is it?'

'The second I stop playing you disappear.'
'That'll be doing both of us a favour.'

The music came to an abrupt halt.

~ ✦ ~

Malachi's room was cold and the only light present, was emitted from the screen of his laptop.

He eyed the email from Sae-Hee Ryong. While his fingers itched to slam the laptop shut, a small part of him wanted to reply, but then again, he didn't want to leave this stranger hanging on the same string he had often been left at. So, he replied.

But not for her — he replied for himself.

~ ✦ ~

Malachi Elakrab <malakrab@gmail.com>
8:43 PM

Bello Sae Hee,

Thank you for your email and your concern.
A touching gesture.
Remington mentioned you in his letters… and yeah, we got the letters.

I don't have a Snapchat and I know that sounds odd.
My photography won't live up its praise and neither will I.

Good luck with university, and I know its not my place to say this, but lay off the coffee.

~M.E.

After sending out the email Malachi laid supine in his bed.

All he craved was silence but Vince's words were being sung by the vicious choir in his mind. He wanted time to stand still and everything to fall into place. He didn't want to fall apart.

The ringing of his phone brought some life to the palace of mannequins. Out of curiosity he glanced at the piece of glass and metal that held most of his life together — after all, the only people that would call him were on his couch, dead asleep. An unknown number greeted him. Malachi ignored the ringing and continued to stare out at the night sky. He sat peacefully on the rather comfortable chair placed on his balcony with his cup of coffee in hand.

The sky was silent and the stars were hidden but his view was lit by the garden lights and the décor for the coming day, and his neighbours' elegant lanterns brought life to his view. The serene atmosphere was occasionally disrupted by the occasional zipping of a vehicle.

People were probably rushing home or away.

The ringing started again and it was the same number.

Malachi huffed at the caller's persistence and reluctantly took the call.

'Hello, is this Malachi?' The Quasar's polite and bubbly voice greeted him.

Why was she calling at this hour? Better yet, why was she calling? She couldn't care that much about the project, could she?

'How did you get my number?' Malachi cut to the chase before taking another sip of his inviting coffee.
'A magician never reveals her secrets.'

Bright.

'*I'm sorry for calling at such an odd hour but I was concerned about you,*' she matched up to his blunt response.
'Apparently you aren't the only one,' Malachi muttered.

He *really* didn't mean to say that out loud.

'I'm sorry,' he apologised almost immediately, 'my social filter is off,' he offered with a weak smile which she couldn't see.

'*It's okay,*' she laughed, '*I don't blame you.*'

Yup, still bright in the dead of night.

'I'm okay,' he murmured, 'sorry for getting you all worked up.'

Why did she care?

'*Are you sure?*'
'Yeah.'
'*You know…*' she trailed off, '*when people say that they are okay they are, most of the time not okay?*'
'This is not one of those times.'
'*If you say so,*' she hummed, but they both knew that he was lying.

Malachi's parents arrived in the dead of night but they didn't sleep. Instead they inspected the decorations and the set-up for the brunch tomorrow. He often felt bad for them, but more often than not he didn't see them to express said sympathy.

Malachi glanced at his watch restlessly noting that there were merely six hours till the guests arrived. At this point he wasn't sure who his parents had invited. He knew that the Simmons and the Johnsons were going to be there come what and may. The Supernova's parents travelled a lot so they had consistently turned down the invite and the Supernova himself rarely showed up. The rest of the guests however, were rather iffy people and the guest list itself kept on changing as per the event but *this brunch* was more intimate than the others.

Since this event was more of family and friends than the other gatherings, he found himself getting more worried.

~ ✦ ~

Malachi got a wink and a half of sleep which was more than usual and more than everyone else in the palace of mannequins combined.

The palace of mannequins was elegantly decorated and for the first time in a long time, people were present, which caused Malachi to self-consciously fiddle with his hair and twiddle his fingers with his gaze trained to his black converse.

He felt out of place in his own house. The kitchen was bustling and there were people running around like headless chickens. *'Even though things were perfect they could always be better.'* That was the attitude in the palace of mannequins.

From the kitchen Malachi could see the garden which seemed like it had been shipped from a fairytale. The usually empty garden had now been dusted with the last spark of dying star. The pool was lit from within and seemingly represented the sunset. There lay a huge mahogany table on the cobblestoned patio... perhaps the food would be placed there? The underground LED lights which followed the stone pathway that lead straight to the pool weren't on yet. The willow trees which served as a natural cover from the neighbour's view into the backyard had fairy lights weaving through the branches. The bright Calla Lilies hid the fences while trapping the lawn with their embrace.

Malachi remembered the day his mother succeeded in convincing his father that they didn't need a Japanese Zen-garden themed backyard. However, there was an indoor garden of sorts which very much had a full-fledged zen garden, a koi pond, and a life-size bamboo fountain.

Malachi loved both of them even though they were a *bit* much. Besides, the backyard explained his parents best. His mother represented sophistication while his father represented the calm. Together they fell into place even though seemingly random.

~ ◆ ~

The guests came in one after the other and they were received by Malachi's parents while Malachi himself gave them a simple smile, engaging in conversation as and when required.

The Lonely Astronaut who had flecks of paint on her both her blue top and white pants, was bickering with the North Star. They had left at some point in the night and come back with their parents.

Malachi swiftly greeted their parents, dreading the arrival of any more guests even though only thirteen had arrived.

The Supernova walked in alone with an infectious smile and the four teenagers engaged formalities with the swiftly arriving adults, and robotically answered the generic questions that followed. Narrowly escaping when new guests walked in.

'Why do they ask the same questions every time?' the Lonely Astronaut grumbled.

'Because knowing anything more than that scares them,' the Supernova mused.

The adults murmured something along the lines of the lack of the Remingtons and slipped away from the sensitive topic. Unfortunately, before the whole ordeal came to an end the Lonely Astronaut managed to convince Malachi's parents to let Malachi go with her, the North Star and the Supernovas, to Vince's place.

~ ◆ ~

daydream

A warm little blanket, from harsh-cold reality.
Save me from misery,
I do not want to go down with your gravity.

I wish I could fly in your beautiful skies,
Take me away from all these lies.
No more reasons to be a part of their schemes.
Let me be wrapped up in daydreams.

I have no need to be one of them,
After all, amongst coal is where you find the brightest gem.
Broken and bent I'm out of shape.
They tried to shut me up with their tape.

I am no longer on that sinking boat.
All I see is their carnage afloat.
Daydreams, you are keeping me afloat.

~ ✦ ~

Chapter 13

whishful thinking

To the stars,

i was spineless.

i don't want a life full of regrets.

i'll try my best

~idyllically, Malachi.

~ ✦ ~

The trio featuring a very reluctant Malachi drove to Vince's place. Malachi didn't hate the drive for two reasons:

1. It was surprisingly rather short so he didn't have time to overthink.

2. Silence couldn't suffocate him in a car full of people.

Malachi did not want to see Vince, let alone go to his house — but he would do it. After all — *'their happiness lies in the balance with you.'*

The day seemed fragmented. Almost like the fractured hearts and broken minds sitting in Vince's living room. When the light hit their fragments, their hidden pain became iridescent yet remained hidden while they showed the world their monochrome shells.

Malachi could see the elements were scattered on the floor representing different levels of sleep deprivation. Fire was sitting with her laptop while leaning against the couch. Her signature black bow lay comfortably on her soft brown hair while her grey trench coat

101

loosely covered her small frame. It seemed like she was explaining something to Water. Across them sat Air and Earth who were laughing and passing comments about the duo in front of them. Even though they were exhausted they seemed content.

Even though their meeting was an accident — beautiful nonetheless — it all made sense when you saw the bright smiles they shared while exchanging their inside jokes.

Surprisingly, the Halley's Comet was laying across the couch with a grey gravity blanket haphazardly placed on her. Vince greeted the trio featuring a reluctant Malachi with a brilliant smile. His hair was now jet-black which seemed almost natural.

'Greetings and welcome to the unconventional and accidental support group for the students of Noctem Arch Academy, the home of the phoenix,' Vince called out while everyone acknowledged the newcomers.
'Cut the theatrics,' Fire scoffed.
'Rich coming from you Anders,' Air laughed before turning to Vince, 'I believe we were promised food.'
'It'll be here in five minutes,' the host pacified him while Fire scowled.

The Lonely Astronaut placed herself on the floor and began talking to Fire and Air. The North Star and Earth were already laughing about something. The Supernova and Water were functioning on a different tangent entirely, gesturing dramatically while Vince found himself trying to wake up the Halley's Comet.

Malachi faded away into the background.

He quietly clicked a picture of the scene before him — maybe the insomniac would like to see this? Malachi didn't know why he was trying to justify his actions to himself.

Then he continued to fade away.

The water rose higher and higher as his feet struggled to remember the ground; he could feel himself beginning to float away. In the darkness he realised that it wasn't water that surrounded him anymore.

It was space, a dark and empty abyss.

'Malachi? You okay?' Probably the Supernova, but his voice sounded distant and faded.
'I agree,' his response was mechanical but quite obviously wrong.
'Bud, A+ on the timely response but your answer kinda sorta missed the mark,' Earth supplied.
'By a mile,' the North Star chipped in.
'Cool.'

'Okay — I think we've lost Malachi,' Air quipped.
'I don't think we ever had him,' Water mused while placing his dark sunglasses near his laptop.

'Why are the lot of you always one-upping me?'
'It comes naturally,' Fire shrugged.
The Lonely Astronaut made her way to the statue that resembled her cousin and waved her hands in front of his face, and just like that, Malachi was back.

'Welcome back!!'

'Malachi, come sit down,' Fire called whilst flipping Air off.

In the haphazard mess of people Malachi found a place between the Supernova and Water, they seemed sane.
The volatile duo was taking digs at each other while simultaneously helping each other and engaging in general conversation. Malachi could not fathom how they managed to stay afloat.

'I'm still waiting on the food that I was promised.'
'You ate two sandwiches less than half an hour ago!!'
'I'm starving René,' he pouted. 'I get irritable when I'm hungry.'
'You are perpetually irritable and there are seven grammatical errors in the first three lines itself.'
'I am not,' he groaned burying his face in his hands. 'Can you fix them?'
'As if,' she heaved a sigh while passing his laptop back to him. 'Fixed

it.'

'Thank you, drama queen.'

'Why, you're quite welcome hoover.'

'Did you just call me a hoover?' Air squawked indignantly at Fire's response and promptly began typing again.

'She did, get your ears checked you crazy-eyed trashcan,' the exasperation was evident in Earth's voice. The dig referenced to Air's peculiar habit of wearing different coloured lenses every day.

'Trashcan? You guys are just jealous of my metabolic rate,' he paused, 'the derivative is wrong.' He passed the book back to Water.

'You know what a metabolic rate is?'

'Don't get ahead of yourself Rosie.'

Fire and Water rebuked at the same time.

An organized mess.

'You bicker like an old married couple,' the Lonely Astronaut observed while typing away on Vince's laptop.

'Don't insult me like that.'

'Like I'd ever end up with the likes of him.'

They valued their friendship too much to throw it away on a whim.

'Can we not go down this road again?' Water muttered with a distinct look in his eye.

'Again?'

'They had a structured debate once which ended with Rosie here whining about the fact that René had an advantage.'

'Well she did!'

'My vast vocabulary isn't an advantage,' Fire snapped. 'However, your inability to articulate your thoughts is a disadvantage.'

'There she goes again.'

'Read a book.'

Vince and the Lonely Astronaut rolled their eyes and continued working on his laptop while the Supernova took over awaking the still-asleep Halley's Comet.

The clacking of the keys and Supernova's soft voice played in the background.

Everyone seemed content. The dark hollows under their eyes told a different story as they worked or just enjoyed the unconventional peace.

In that moment he realised that the light that made their fragments iridescent came from their effervescent smiles. Malachi found himself being pulled towards the hidden smiles behind the sharp insults being thrown around.

'I don't see the point of your grand piano Vince,' Air pointed out while stretching his neck.
'It's useless, just like him,' a now-awake Halley's Comet supplied.
'You know I liked you better when you were unconscious, Delia,' Vince muttered while running his hands through his hair.

'Then why'd you wake me up Mafler?'
'It was Arthur.'
'You tried to before him.'

Vince shot her an offended look and dramatically placed his hands on his heart.

'Malachi can play the piano.' Malachi decided that he too liked the Halley's Comet better when she was unconscious.

'Really?'
'Why would someone lie about that, you nimrod?'

'Do you two ever stop bickering?'

'She started it!'
'My bad, six-year-old.'

'You seriously don't see the resemblance?' The Supernova mused while nudging the Lonely Astronaut.
'What resemblance? There is nothing to see,' she scoffed but the

whisper of a smile on her lips told a whole other story.

The North Star glowered at the Supernova while Vince flipped him off.

'Can you play something for us?' Earth's baritone voice silenced his distracted friends.

It made sense that the North Star and Earth clicked, they resonated with each other's misery of taking care of children which weren't even theirs to begin with.

Malachi froze — he didn't want to meet Kamaria again but he didn't know how to say no.
'Sure.'

Malachi reluctantly stood up and made his way to the piano in the corner of the living room. As he walked across the threshold, he absorbed Vince's house. Which was black and white with not a single drop of colour.

'The lot of you,' The Halley's Comet hollered while pushing her short black hair into her face to shield her freckles, 'Shut up or get out.'

Silence prevailed once again.

And then the dulcet sound of the soft melody danced in the air. Malachi watched as his fingers danced to the symphony they had created. The room faded away and a set of familiar hands joined his.

Kamaria.

The music got sweeter.

'New friends I see,' she stated matter-of-factly.
'Glorified acquaintances,' he whispered, 'they won't last for long.'
'We'll see about that,' she hummed.
'Sure.'

'Malachi, who I am in your universe?'
'Stardust,' he said almost instantly.

'Huh? I'm *space dust*?'
'No... technically yes but-'

'No, I'm stardust.'

He blinked twice at her response.

'I'm the remnants of something beautiful.'
'What?'
'Malachi, I'm remnants of the broken fragments of your mind.'

Malachi froze, but his fingers kept on dancing.

The Lonely Astronaut, the North Star, the Supernova and Vince leaned back and enjoyed the music while the Halley's Comet rested on her side on the couch, facing the obsidian-haired pianist. The ethereal elements however were gawking at Malachi. Air's eye was twitching while his restless fingers bothered both his industrial and upper lobe piercings. Fire was opening and closing her mouth like a fish — Malachi was surprised that the duo hadn't thrown insults at each other's unflattering reactions. Earth was buffering and Water looked like he was trying to find *Waldo*.

The music was slowly swallowed by the sanguine silence which caused the elements to break into applause. Malachi smiled shyly as he unconsciously made his way back to the group.

'Dude, you are ridiculously talented,' Earth exclaimed with genuine awe flashing in his warm eyes.
'Thank you.'

'On a support group-ish tangent,' Vince flashed the Supernova an impish grin. 'How is the project for Mr Salone's class coming along Delia?'

Mt. Blue promptly blew up.

'Arthur!' she screeched, 'we still haven't started.' The Halley's Comet sprung up from the couch and glared at the student body president who was glaring at Vince.

'We'll get there,' he promised.
'You've been saying that for two weeks now.'

'Ha!' Vince scoffed, 'Acenath and I have closed on our topic Delia, when will you ever catch up?'
'Arthur!' she screeched, menacingly looming over the fair-haired boy, 'we have to finish before them.'
'You can't rush perfection.'
'Watch me,' the Halley's Comet raised her chin defiantly with a look of determination in her eyes.

'Wait-wait-wait, you took two weeks to close on the topic?' The North Star's concern was evident.
'No,' Vince paused, 'we took three weeks.'
'That's way better, Mafler,' Fire laughed while the bow on her pixie cut hair shook wildly but refused to fall.

'I'm just glad I'm not in whatever this class is,' The North Star heaved a sigh of relief and the elements followed suit.
'The education system is a joke,' The Halley's Comet declared.
'It is, isn't it?'
'As much as I'd like to get into this,' he paused, 'I don't want to do this on an empty stomach.' Shooting daggers at Vince with his violet eyes.
'It's on its way.'
'From where? The south pole?'

Vince rolled his eyes but made no move to go check on the food.

'Pipe down Rosie,' Water chided while subconsciously running his fingers on the scar that ran from under his right year till his collar bone.
'Don't call me that,' there was no traceable amount of venom in his voice.
'My bad Trashcan,' he apologised, 'do you prefer hoover, Rosie?'

Fire raised her hand for a high-five.
Water did not leave her hanging even for a nano-second.
'Rosie?'
'She hacked apart his last name.'

The Lonely Astronaut added fuel to the flame of the ongoing battle between Fire and Air to which Water chipped in every now then, however he mostly found himself rethinking his life choices with a lazy smirk. The Supernova sat there highly amused.

An unnatural silence prevailed but there was nothing uncomfortable.

Malachi stood in the present.

The voices were soft but this time they had a different train of thought.

'This feels nice.'

'This is probably a one-time thing.'

'DO NOT GET USED TO THIS.'

'Once they see what you really are, they'll leave.'

'Just another group of people you will end up hurting.'

Nope, they were back.

'Will we ever be good enough?' The Halley's Comet's question instantly brought silence to the once chaotic-room.

'Who knows?' The North Star barely whispered back.

'With our parents' unreasonable standards, even if I may be good enough, I sure as hell won't feel it,' Water sighed.

'Can we not go down this road?' Vince pleaded whilst throwing a pillow at the Halley's Comet which she easily deflected.

'The road of *'it's just a phase'*? Phase they say, the last five years of my life aren't a phase,' Parker bit back.

From the unrelenting tides Malachi could see a glimmer.

Water isn't only found in the oceans of the world but also the oases of relief, the joy of the first rain, and a tear of pain.

The waters may be home for some mysterious horrors of the world but every now and then the cycle of chaos breaks. The lulling calm of the waves is like the songs of the sirèns, which remind us of the lost treasures and cities.

Water.

Parker Darrow, the boy with layers more intriguing than the levels of hell.
An added coat to hide every ounce of damage done.
When the light hits, the fractured layers glitter.
Parker Darrow stood in the prism.
Imprisoned.

'New topic! Where is the food?'

Everyone in the room exchanged a look, and Earth and Fire frisbeed pillows onto the head on the boy in the overalls with numerous piercings, violet eyes and a huge smile.

~ ✦ ~

halcyon memories that we destroy

To the stars,

It seems as though the whole world has been lied to; we all dream of a 'happy ever after'. But forget right after those words comes 'THE END'.

Conveniently we all ignore this.

The new week is a stranger; in fact, the new hour, the new minute, and the new second are all strangers during which we make memories. In some we meet and befriend strangers, and in others we watch as people become strangers.

It's a strange exchange to watch in strange times.

It's good to know that I have one person in my life who is not a stranger. I don't think I'd be able to live to see the day you fade away — a stranger with the name of someone I love.

~Liberosis, Remington.

~ ◆ ~

The walk home was slow; the world seemed to fade away and the lights made him dizzy. Malachi's legs felt heavy and every fibre of his being was hurting, but this was better than the suffocating silence in his car. He rejected pretty much everyone's offer to drop him home with a polite smile.

He didn't want to be a burden.

More often than not, in the middle on the night, embarrassing memories flashed in his head on a never-ending loop. Maybe that could be a form of second-hand embarrassment? Malachi was a victim to this evil far too much.

The middle of the night was seemingly the best time to reminisce the past.

Intentionally or unintentionally.

Malachi did not want to cry. He could feel the tears threatening to spill, struggling to hold himself together, he yearned to throw himself onto his bed. The soft mattress had been tainted by so many of his tears.

He had no idea how he had ended up here.

Alone.

Things finally felt like they were working out, and now it felt like his whole world was falling apart. Having no idea if he was lying to himself the whole day to feel some illusion of happiness. *Maybe it was real?*

'Will I ever be good enough?' he relayed the question from the unconventional get-together.

He quickened his step as he walked up to the porch. Behind his closed eyelids he could see the flashes of everyone who surrounded him leaving.

He felt guilt.

Other people have it worse and here he was whining about his life. Malachi wondered if things could ever get worse. What would he do if things got worse?

Would he end it all? Take the easy way out? Was there an easy way out?

Malachi lived in the future surrounded by fear. His being yearned for relief, and the sound of silence around him served as a constant reminder that no one was around to care.

Malachi wanted to feel human again.

He was tired of being numb.
He hated the numbness after the hours of pain.

It was a like a vicious cycle that blended itself together into a never-ending song.
It was like a screeching in his veins.

His own private hell.

'A phase,' his breathy voice broke the silence in his room.

Nothing was really a phase until it ended and this was an ongoing battle that took no name of ending.

It will end with me.

Malachi was swallowed by the darkness and there was no light.
In the distance he could see the Lonely Astronaut and the North Star calling out to him.

But he was slipping away.

There were so many bright bodies of light around him.
Yet he couldn't see them.

The darkness around him had manifested into a swinging blade. The darkness had entered his lungs and he was choking on the blade of relief which twisted painfully in his lifeless vessel.

An uneasy panic flooded his drowning mind and he called out for help.
His voice muffled as he drowned.
His hands and legs were tied to the anchor that continued to aid in sinking him.

He wanted to let go and accept the darkness.
He often wondered what it would be like to give up.
He was tired of fighting.

But a part of him was terrified — hopeful even, he didn't want to go back to what had been, but he didn't want to suffer this way.

Maybe this was it.

The end?

~ ✦ ~

Malachi walked to the kitchen through the dimly lit hallway. Although his eyes had adjusted to the darkness the silence was enveloping him.

He could hear the silence.
It was calming and warm.

A comfortable silence.

He stood in front of the refrigerator across the marble island.
Ping.

The silence was back.

Malachi glanced at his phone; it was an email from the insomniac that Malachi opened almost instantly.

~ ✦ ~

Sae Hee Ryong <ryongsaehee@gmail.com>
10:37 PM

To me.

Dear Malachi Elakrab,

Bello! Yay! I'm so happy you replied.

I'm sorry for the late reply… university isn't all bells and whistles. It's a well-thought-out trap for all the innocent people who want a higher education. In exchange for money, energy, efforts, and our souls, we may get a job. I'm 10000000000000% sure you and your pictures will live up to the praise. Eros was hardly ever wrong.

CREATE A SNAPCHAT ACCOUNT!

I'm never going to lay off coffee.
It is impossible.

I'm having a mid-morning dance party.

~Ryong Sae-Hee.

~ ✦ ~

Malachi couldn't help but smile at the email.
Coffee.
Malachi decided he wanted coffee.

~ ✦ ~

Malachi Elakrab <malakrab@gmail.com>
10:44 PM

Bello Sae Hei,

Thank you for going on with my typo and enjoy your mid-morning dance party.
If I reach that level of boredom, I may create a snapchat account.

…. I actually clicked a picture (today) and it's attached below.

~M.E.

~ ✦ ~

Something about the enigma on the other side pulled him in. Her words were entrancing and her essence jumped out through her words.

Just like Eros said.

That night Malachi created a Snapchat account.

Malachi looked at the image that greeted him.
Sae-Hee Ryong.
Magnetic.
A Black Hole.

Sipping his iced coffee Malachi made his way back to his room. Sae-Hee had to go for her morning lecture, not before adding Malachi as a friend on Snapchat. She sent him a snap.

His first snap.

A front camera video of the Black Hole's pitch-black hair with the soft shadow of a bright purple danced with her, in front of her alluring smile and shining eyes. The caption: 'mid-morning dance party.'

There was something alluring about her.

Malachi, however, had sent a what-he-later-learnt, was a blank snap.

'Can I call you?' Came her message.

Malachi hesitated and the second he sent his message he was getting a video call via Snapchat.

'Bello!' the Black hole on the other end greeted him.
'Bello,' he laughed.

'Why did you send me a blank snap?' she asked while exiting presumably her dorm room.

'Show me more of your photography,' she declared while pushing her shining hair out of her face. 'Eros never shut up about it.'
'Really?'
'Yeah, obviously,' she laughed, *'never showed me anything though,'* she complained with a pout.

He smiled at her reaction and looked for one of his albums.

'*Your eyes are so pretty,*' she cooed at Malachi who was now hiding his blush behind his hair.

He found the picture of the twins playing their instruments the night before the school festival. He flipped the camera and showed her the picture.

'*Woah, Eros wasn't kidding.*'
'Thank you.'
'*Why are you thanking me? I should be thanking you for showing me this beautiful piece of art.*'
'Thank you.'
'*Again, with the thank you. Now I've finally got a streak worth my time,*' She paused, '*I can tell why Eros was in love with you.*'

Malachi froze.

'*Is the screen frozen?*' she asked confused.

When Malachi blinked, she laughed, '*But let's not get into that,*' she waved her hand, '*I want to know more about you.*'
'Why? I'm not that great.' Malachi muttered while noticing the background around her change to a blue-grey sky.
'*You are too harsh on yourself.*'
'How are you so sure?'
'*I'm a law student, I will be the judge of things.*'
'Don't you have a morning lecture to get to?'

She made a face at him and began running towards the lecture which had completely slipped her mind.

Malachi found it easy to talk to her.
He couldn't stop talking to her.

~ ◆ ~

His room felt cold but it still felt like a warm embrace when compared to the iced coffee. The warm, deep blue blankets cocooned around him almost perfectly — well they were made for him... so they kinda had to.

Malachi looked at his neighbours' glittering backyard through his French windows. The glittering lights dimmed the whispering stars above. A loud explosion from the skies followed by a streak of light marked the beginning of the heavy downpour, and just like that, it was the stormiest of nights. The skies roared unleashing their pent-up anger. Flashes of lightning slashed back at the skies, it seemed as if the forces of nature were battling to show their power and dominant sides; the lightning's sword clashing against the sky's midnight black shield. It wasn't the only battle that took place that night.

Malachi's eyes watched the ongoing battle, he *almost* missed a call from the Quasar.

'I'm glad that you took my call,' she paused. *'But why are you awake at this ungodly hour?'*

He scoffed, getting comfortable in his cocoon.
'You do realise that I can't do both those things at the same time, right?'
'Touché.'

'Besides, why are you awake?'
'So many questions, such little time.'

A bright flash followed by a growl of fury sounded from the sky. The wind's whistling became louder and more unforgiving, making the trees sway and the leaves rustle in an attempt to stay with their branches.

'I hope our school is shut tomorrow.'
'It's on a hill.'
'If Jack and Jill went tumbling down the hill then so will I.'
'Tomorrow's a Sunday.'
'Oh… yeah.'
'Besides I thought you liked school.'
'I'm not that far gone.'

Malachi hummed condescendingly and took another sip of his coffee. Something felt different about their conversation this time — it was almost too comfortable.

'What did you do today?'
'My parents had their monthly get-together today.'
'That sounds like fun!!'
'It's really not,' he muttered with pain evident in his voice.

'Is it usually that bad?'
'No.'
'What changed?' she paused before quickly adding, *'That is if you don't mind me asking.'*
'Nothing really.'

As his answers grew shorter, he could see what had happened. Malachi had walked into a trap with his eyes wide open.

'Holding things in isn't healthy.'

Then again, what about Malachi was healthy?

He merely hummed.

'You can talk to me about it if you want.'
'I'll keep that in mind.'

The battle in the sky was slowly coming to an end and the whistling winds were reduced to a whisper. Silence returned but this time there was nothing comforting about it.

Who would have thought that the bright and pleasant Quasar would be capable of laying such a trap?
Wait, you know what, that makes sense.
Maybe she was being nice so far to hide her evil plan?
Her evil plan to be a nice person?

She's literally on the phone right now and you haven't said anything for a few minutes. That's your cue to say something.
Say something!!!

'So…'

Kudos to you, bud. You started a sentence! Now articulate your thoughts and finish the damned sentence.

'So…'

Wow! Would you look at that? She's just as bad as you.

Malachi's brain was melting, the choir in his head was usually more brutal and struck him where they knew it would hurt. This time however, there was a new tone to the malicious chorus. This particular chorus woke up whenever he spoke to the Quasar.

'Do you think happiness runs away from us?' The words flew out of her mouth, almost naturally.

'No,' he paused, 'but sometimes I find myself thinking if I've used up all the joy in my life and all that is left to feel is sadness.'

Time stopped.

'But every now and then the people around me stop me from fading away and I feel guilty for questioning my happiness.'
'Because our happiness comes from people.'

Silence.

'I wonder why we give them so much power,' she laughed. *'But we do, and all we can do is hope that they aren't going to take all the light out of our lives when they leave.'*

The Quasar.
Her smile was the blinding light at the end of the tunnel.

Most minds run to the Sun when thinking of light and they forget that the Quasar's elysian nature heals and entrances.

Talon Davis, the embodiment of the fractured light that glows with a thousand colours dancing through the windows of a cold room.

'So, Malachi Elakrab, who took the light out of your life?'

'Remington.'

Her silence asked him to continue.

'I let him go and he came back — but death got in the way.'
'Malachi-'

'He was a year older than us and he was my best friend,' he smiled fondly. 'He was perfect and I know they say that no one can be perfect — but even his flaws were beautiful,' he heaved a sigh. 'His presence made the world make sense.

'I could never love myself when waking up itself reminded me of my failures — one day the voices got too loud, and I couldn't control them. So, I ignored them. I ignored them and they swallowed me whole.'

And then the words began flowing out.

'Turns out that he was in love with me,' Malachi stared at the stars with an empty smile.

'Did you-'
'I don't know.' Malachi answered honestly, 'And that is what scares me the most — someone who meant that much to me — and I don't even know if I loved him.

'Maybe at some point I did—but now I can't tell anymore because every time something reminds me of him I slip into my mind—I can't find anything that wasn't tainted.'

'I destroyed everything; I tore apart the same memories I wish I could relive because I was weak, and even now everyone is still trying to protect me.'

'Ma-'

But he cut the call before she could say anything.
He didn't want sympathy.
He didn't know why told her everything to begin with.

~ ◆ ~

illogical justified heartache

to the stars,

i think i'm making a friend.

i think.

~idyllically, Malachi

~ ✦ ~

In the days Malachi had spent locked away in his room with a broken spirit and a fractured mind, numb to the world he once floated around in, he learnt that the world moves on, people move on. No matter how much they care and cry, they move on.

They move on with or without you.

Malachi had decided that he was tired of being left behind.

He was tired of having life pass him by while he tried to understand the world around him — the same world that didn't care about him. Sure, some people cared and went out of their way... but for how long? How long until you only feel guilty about no longer caring? How long until that guilt is gone? How long until that spark goes away and you just smile at the memories that come in flashes?

~ ✦ ~

The Lonely Astronaut was driving around aimlessly in her oversized sweatshirt and black jeans.

It's not like anyone cares where I am.

It was only behind the wheel where she had control.

Her pastel hair carelessly danced with the wind in the night sky, while she felt like she was being weighed down by the worries of the world.

Finding herself at the beach she pulled over and stared blankly at the water. The black waves lashing against the grey sands eased her, the moon's bright reflection on the waters made her look up at the stars. After the storm, the looming clouds had disappeared and everything around her felt electric.

A smile made its way to her face and memories flashed before her eyes with the waves singing to her flashbacks.

'Eros, how am I supposed to be strong for him? When I'm broken,' her voice cracked and her throat began to tingle as she held back her tears. 'Devon can't stay strong for the both of us forever... we were always broken but you held us together.

'How do I feel whole again?' She closed her eyes feeling them burn with unshed tears.

'If you were here you'd hold us and you'd know exactly what to say — FUCK! Why am I crying?' she yelled to the skies.

'I miss you — and if I'm this bad then how bad is he?' she sniffled. 'You always said that he's stronger than the lot of us put together... but- but he's *Malachi*.'

She threw her head back and held her pastel locks in her hands.

'One colour for every time I've missed you. I'm going to run out of colours soon,' she laughed while choking on her sobs.

'Please don't leave me. I don't want to forget — I don't want to forget the good, the bad, or the ugly. I know you're gone — but don't leave me — don't leave us-' a sob slipped past her lips. 'Who am I supposed to go to after these drives in the dead of night?'

'Who will tease Devon with me?'

'Who'll play the piano while I sketch?

'Whose bedroom walls am I supposed to practice my new techniques on?'

The tears began running down her face.

'Who will — no one can replace you... you always said that don't close your heart to the rest of the world — but how can I open my heart to the world when I can't face it?

'Remember Vince? He's so worried about all of us and so is Arthur. But they're just watching us disintegrate and the pieces seem too small to be put together again.'

~ ✦ ~

The North Star was baking.

In the dead of night, he was whipping buttercream for the cupcakes baking in the oven behind him.

He was an artist in the kitchen, much like his grandmother, with the dream of making everyone who tasted his food feel loved and accepted.

But his critic was the toughest.

You said you'd be the first to eat at my restaurant — how were we supposed to know this would happen?

He continued mixing the frosting, his movements calm and composed while his brain was overflowing.

How am I supposed to be strong for them?

He began filling the piping bag.

I'm sorry I couldn't bring myself to speak at your funeral — But I knew if I started crying, I wouldn't stop and then who would take care of Malachi and Acenath?

Ding!

He wasn't worried about the sound, it's not like there was anyone at home who would get disturbed to begin with. His parents had taken a flight out to Kenya about an hour ago to visit his grandmother.

He set the cupcakes on the cooling rack and walked over to the huge French widows that overlooked his pool. The lights in the garden reflected on the pool and he smiled as the tears ran down his face.

He began pacing around the room aimlessly. He had never felt this helpless in his own life.

His brain couldn't come up with a solution.

He racked his brains but his head was aching.
He hadn't slept in weeks and every time sleep would come to him, he'd shove her away.

If they're crying themselves to sleep... why do I deserve sleep? He couldn't grieve, if he did, who would be their support system?

Malachi's ringing phone broke the silence in his room.

The Lonely Astronaut.

He blinked twice and took her call.

'We're at the gate, let us in.'
'Sure.'

Malachi made his way through the mansion of mannequins to the front gate where the Lonely Astronaut's black jeep stood at attention. He punched in the code and stood off to the side as the door opened and the Lonely Astronaut's car strode in. While Malachi punched in the code to close the gate the car's windows rolled down.

The North Star waved at the curly-haired boy; the Lonely Astronaut called, 'Get in.'

Malachi nodded and hopped onto the backseat. The car drove up to the porch and the Lonely Astronaut parked at her designated spot. They hopped out and silently made their way into the mansion of mannequins, their soft footsteps sounded like thunder in the silence. It didn't seem like they knew where they were going but eliminated every room as they walked pass it.

The trio soon found themselves back on the front lawn.

Neither the North Star nor the Lonely Astronaut passed a comment about the fruitless, walk but deep down they all knew that they all needed time to get their thoughts together. The Lonely Astronaut sat down on the dry, shaded patio, with her legs stretched out onto the damp and slightly mucky lawn. She stared blankly at the sky.

'I miss him.'
Malachi's breath hitched.

'Every day I'd wake up and think it would hurt less with a new day,' she swallowed gravely. 'I don't want to stop missing him.'

I don't want to forget him.

The unsaid words danced around the trio.

'How've you been?' Malachi barely whispered.

'I've been getting by.'

They hadn't looked each other in eye yet.
How could they?
'I miss us,' Malachi whispered.

The Lonely Astronaut smiled and closed her eyes to hold back her tears while the North Star looked down at his feet to hide his.

'He's really gone, isn't he?'

Yes.

'Why him?' Malachi muttered and joined the Lonely Astronaut on the patio.

Why not me?

'You've read the letters, right?' The North Star croaked.
'Yeah.'

'I miss us too,' the Lonely Astronaut whimpered and Malachi froze when he watched tears run down her illuminated skin.

'I'm sorry,' the North Star whispered and joined the duo on the patio.

'You aren't expected to get through this alone,' the Lonely Astronaut stated to no one in particular.
'None of you have to be strong for me,' Malachi's voice finally broke. 'Why do you have to put on your brave faces and pretend everything is okay for me?'

'Please don't do that,' he barely managed to get the last sentence out.

'I have no idea what brave face you are talking about. I haven't stopped crying since that day,' the North Star broke the silence.

'I – I'm just playing a part in a world I can't begin to understand. I don't want to worry the others but every now and then I feel happy; genuine happiness and then I feel guilt.'

'You are allowed to heal, Ace.'
'I can't when guilt is eating me alive.'
'You can let other people in... our happiness comes from people Ace.'

Malachi felt like a hypocrite.

'Happiness?' The Lonely Astronaut turned to look at her cousin who was fiddling with his fingers.

'You feel guilty about healing but — but healing doesn't mean you stop missing him or stop caring about him or you've replaced him,' he turned to her with glassy eyes. 'It just means you are healing.'

Acenath looked at her cousin and finally understood why Eros had said he was stronger than the lot of him put together. Because he was strong enough to face the truth even with his sensitive nature.

She smiled and leaned forward to hug him. She began sobbing into their embrace. Devon let out a watery laugh and the duo turned to stare at their Moral Compass.

'I'm sorry I wasn't strong enough for us.'

The tears ran down his cheeks and the trio held onto each other like their lives depended on it.

They trio had grown up together.
They feared growing apart.

In that moment time stood still. The world didn't pass them by and there they lay feeling every blocked emotion. The floodgates had been opened. Every single emotion that they had shielded themselves from was now slipping into their lives.

~ ✦ ~

'So, why'd you colour your hair?' Malachi asked while fidgeting with Acenath's multi-coloured locks.

'Teenage rebellion?' Devon guessed.

'It's not teenage rebellion, but after the accident I needed some colour in my life... so every time I missed him I got a new colour,' she murmured, 'to add some colour to my life.'

'Oh.'

'Even though you have pretty much every colour on your head, Mafler's red hair looked way more messed up,' Devon scoffed.

Acenath laughed and closed her eyes.

'I told him about the stars,' she confessed with a guilty smile.
'You did?' Devon sounded surprised.

'I'm sorry,' she quickly apologised while staring into Malachi's eyes.

'I'm not surprised,' he smiled. Even though Vince wasn't his biggest fan and he didn't really know much about him. His words often rang in his ears and he obviously meant a lot to the duo before him, so he didn't mind it.

They were healing and opening up.

'I'm pretty sure he must have said something to Cordelia just to spite her,' Devon mused.

Malachi laughed at the mention of the duelling captains but that opened another path in his mind.

'I told Talon,' he confessed.
'About the stars?' Devon was surprised yet again.

'Not that.'
'What did she say?' Acenath was curious.
'I don't know,' he smiled sheepishly, 'I cut the call on her before she could say anything.'

Acenath laughed at her cousin's antics while Devon rolled his eyes.

'I also told Arthur about the letter,' his voice became soft. 'Did you know?'
'About what Malachi?'

'...*The letter.*'

Acenath froze and Devon's eye widened.

'No,' Acenath murmured, 'I always had a feeling — but I never knew for sure.'

Eros' confession had thrown the trio into a whirlwind of emotions.

'I could never bring myself to ask him,' Devon heaved a sigh. 'I wish I did.'

Malachi always lived in fear of the future, and now that he could feel those fears melting away, only regret remained.

'To the stars,' they whispered.

simplicity of falling apart

to the stars,

i'm sorry

~idyllically, Malachi

~ ◆ ~

The morning came early.
Maybe a little too early.

But for people who slept at the crack of dawn, the trio couldn't complain.

Acenath drove herself and Devon home the second the black and blue sky had prominent hues of pink and yellow.

Sleep however, did not bother with Malachi.
He couldn't bring himself to sleep and his racing mind did nothing to help his dilemma.

~ ◆ ~

Malachi had no idea how this had happened.

He found himself taking a stroll in the park down the road. He couldn't hear the birds, only the footsteps of the various people walking, running, and jogging on the tracks. He was the only one who could.

Everyone had their earphones on and were running past the world with their favourite songs playing as the background track to their fleeting moments of freedom.

Maybe they were running away from their responsibilities or dreaming about the what ifs. After all, it's fun to fantasise about your ideal future but that makes reality even harsher to face.

Malachi walked under the trees, the soft rustling of their leaves was fading away and not a single person cared. The soft light of the sun danced through the gaps between the branches, creating intricate shadows on the ground. There was a dirt path which was hidden by the Willow trees that marked the beginning of the long track that led to the beach. This often made Malachi wonder who planned the city and what they were on when they did.

'Malachi.'

He turned around to see a familiar face; the Halley's Comet.

He smiled at her.

She smiled at him brightly but there was something in her eyes that he couldn't put his finger on. She grabbed his hand and began running down the dirt path.

He shrieked while his legs struggled to keep up. It seemed as though his body knew that nothing good would come from protesting, besides she was easily the strongest person he knew.

'Run Malachi!' she called while laughing.

He could barely keep up.

'I'm just glad we aren't in water right now!' Malachi called.

She laughed yet again. Malachi didn't know if she was slowing down or he was getting faster but soon they were running side-by-side.

The Halley's Comet was something else.

Malachi could see the beach from the corner of his eye and his burning legs were beyond thrilled at the idea of soon coming to a stop. The Halley's Comet had eyes set straight ahead with a brilliant smile on her face as they slowly came to a stop.

Malachi bent down and was struggling to catch his breath, but for some weird reason he couldn't stop smiling.

'Now wasn't that fun?'

Malachi nodded brightly.

'This is why you should always listen to Cordelia.'
'Did you just refer to yourself in third person?'

She gave him a pointed look, 'Stop being such an Arthur.'

'That's too high an honour.'
She scoffed, 'In which world?'
'Why'd you drag me to the beach?'
'Audere Est Facere,' she merely shrugged.

Malachi blinked twice.

'To do is to dare.'
'Why do you speak Latin?'
'Why do you breathe?'
'It's because I have to,' Malachi squawked indignantly.
'You have to speak Latin?'
'No, but wasn't that a good comeback?'
'It would've been if it made sense.'
'The Merriam-Webster dictionary defines good as... Wouldn't it be cool if I knew exactly what it said?' she laughed again and turned to face Malachi with a glow in her sapphire eyes. 'I dragged you to the beach because you looked like you were fading away in the park,' she chirped.

Fading away.

'You want to go get coffee?' she asked glancing at her watch.

Malachi nodded expecting them to walk back from where they had come.

'Where are you going? My car is there,' she pointed at a deep green car about fifteen meters away.

Right. That makes sense.

Malachi followed the Halley's Comet as she made her way to her car.

Her car was well-kept with a huge gym bag in the backseat. True to her nature, she connected her phone to the speaker before putting on her seatbelt. Satisfied with her selection she put her seatbelt on and began pulling out of her parking spot.

Having not bothered to put the windows up, their obsidian-hair was flailing in the wind and her short hair was no longer shielding her freckles from the rest of the world. She zipped down the street towards the coffee shop while humming along to the song with her eyes set dead on the road ahead. The song came to an abrupt halt and the ringing of her phone surrounded them.

Bloodhound.

The Halley's Comet made a face and she answered the call.

'What do you want?'
'Hello to you too.'

Vince sounded exhausted.

'Hi!' she chirped, 'What do you want?' Her scowl was back but there was not a single ounce of hatred in her eyes.

'You are out of coffee.'
'I'm going to the coffee shop,' she smirked while drumming her fingers on the wheel.
'Okay, so?'
'That means I'm getting my daily dose of caffeine, so the lack of coffee is more of a *you* problem than a *me* problem,' she stuck her tongue out at her phone.

Silence.

'I don't like you very much.'
'I don't really care.'
'Bring an iced coffee for me.'

'Nope,' she sang popping the 'p'.

Malachi opened his mouth-

'Don't you dare Malachi.'
'Malachi is there?'

'No.' Her scowl deepened, 'What is a Malachi?'

'Ha-Ha, real funny,' he deadpanned. *'Malachi can you please get an iced coffee for me?'* His saccharine-sweet voice came through the phone.

Malachi fidgeted in his seat under the Halley's Comet's glare.

'Oh no! We are going through a tunnel,' she called.
'There are no tunn-' She cut the call with a satisfied smile.

'Malachi, when you want a pest to leave your house you don't make it comfortable.'

The way she spoke would make you think that she was telling you the secrets of the universe.

The song continued from where it was interrupted and the Halley's Comet went back to humming when all of a sudden, she began receiving various messages.

'Ping!' **Bloodhound.**
'Ping!' **Bloodhound.**
'Ping!' **Bloodhound.**

The song continued again.

The song came to an abrupt halt yet again; this time the ringing of her phone surrounded them.

Bloodhound.

She cut the call with a determined smile.

'Ping!' **Bloodhound.**
'Ping!' **Bloodhound.**
'Ping!' **Bloodhound.**
'Ping!' **Bloodhound.**
'Ping!' **Bloodhound.**
'Ping!' **Bloodhound.**

This did not deter the Halley's Comet and she continued drumming her fingers to the beat of the ignored notifications. While she danced in her seat Malachi could see the coffee shop from the passenger's seat, the soft grey material was warmer than before.

She promptly drove past the front door of the coffee shop.

Even for a Sunday morning there was still quite a queue at the coffee chop. They shuffled forward like penguins, well, penguins who are ready to sell their soul for caffeine. She pulled up into the drive-through lane, 'I'll take two iced coffees and a rainbow special with extra ice.'

Poor Vince would be getting a liquid rainbow.

As it turned out, Malachi ended up with the liquid rainbow.

He had been home for less than twenty minutes when he found himself lying supine on his bed with his heart beating a million beats per second.

SPINELESS.
STUPID.
WORTHLESS.
SPINELESS.

The soft comforting words of reassurance were completely drowned out by the choir.

'Malachi, honey, you okay?' His mother's concerned voice called out from the other side of the door.

His anxiety cost him this.

He didn't want to lose another person.

He wanted to... to be human again.

He barely managed to walk over to the door.
The knocking had stopped.
He heard his mother sigh.

She was used to not hearing an answer.

He opened the door.

'Honey, you okay?' Came her steady and surprised voice.
'No, I'm not.'

The truth.

She saw his tear-streaked face. His hair was shaggy and messy. The blueish-black bags under his eyes seemed to carry the weight of the world, and stood out out on his ashy complexion.

He looked tired.

She held him as he cried.

'Malachi, what happened?' He wanted to tell her everything but he couldn't bring himself to say a single word.

His tears weren't just his and they weren't just of the now.

For the first time his mother was speechless.
She didn't tell him *'it gets better.'* Or *'you'll be okay.'* Or *'it's just a phase.'*

She knew.

'Malachi?' His father's voice resonated though the walls.

His father froze when he saw his son's crumbled figure in his wife's arms and promptly ran over to them. They held him while he cried his heart out and they didn't question him. They expected this.

But they were surprised they got to witness this.

~ ✦ ~

CHAPTER 17

Plummeting from the Stars

To my dear,

I dreamt of owning a leather-bound notebook, a diary if you may. I dreamt of writing poems and songs in that book which would have been engraved with memories.

I dreamt of pages full of sketches of things I found. Random pictures of moments we value the most.

I dreamt of a book that could hold my heart, a book with constellations and the secrets of the world.

But nothing I did could live up to the dream that resides in my heart.

~Liberosis, Remington.

~ ✦ ~

Chaos.

There was so much chaos around him.

He registered their voices and his surroundings.
He could hear his heartbeat in his ears and dread filling his system.
He could see them wildly gesturing to him but that was it; he couldn't hear what they were saying.

Everything sounded distant.

Unable to process his surroundings he blindly followed them to the car.

Everything sounded distant.

His body was frozen.
His mind was racing.
His world was falling apart.

There was so much chaos around him.

Chaos.

~ ✦ ~

'Malachi, Acenath is in the hospital she-she...'
She got into an accident.

~ ✦ ~

The world was blurry but there was not a single tear in his eye, he ran as fast as he could. Racing through the cold and alien hallways of the hospital, ignoring the staff who asked them to slow or calm down.

Calm down?

In all honesty Malachi had no idea where they were running to, but his parents seemed to have an idea about their destination, and came to an abrupt halt in front of two familiar pacing figures with tears in their eyes. They didn't seem to notice the presence of the Elakrabs who were trying to catch their breaths.

Malachi threw himself onto his unsuspecting aunt who registered the presence of the Elakrabs and held her nephew.

~ ✦ ~

The Lonely Astronaut had broken a few of her ribs which punctured her lungs, nearly fractured her skull and she had broken her right arm. Although stabilized, she was still in the ICU with various flowers and cards by her bed.

Malachi watched as people came and went and as the flowers slowly began to wilt. It had been three days since the accident and Malachi had not left the hospital since, but he couldn't bring himself to go in and see her.

The North Star and the Supernova came on the day itself.
The Halley's Comet and the Meteorite came on the first day.
The Elements and The Aurora Borealis came on the second day.

The Quasar came in the last half an hour of the visiting hours on the third day, and Malachi was sent home an hour after her visit.

None of them had shed a tear, neither had Malachi — they refused to cry because that meant accepting reality.

He had finally found it in him to face the world and to look people in the eye, but now he didn't know if he would be able to do the same again.

He was okay with the world passing him by.

The North Star drove him to school on the fourth day but Malachi couldn't even bother to put on a mask or even try. The North Star didn't look any better; his eyes were bloodshot and his uniform was crumpled. Not a single word was uttered through the journey, only the soft hum of the car gliding through traffic.

Everyone in the pristine glass building gave them looks of pity and every time someone tried to approach them, they ran away or walked right through them. They spent most of their time in the lab avoiding human interaction.

On the fifth day, the Lonely Astronaut woke up and the first thing she did was cry.

~ ◆ ~

'I almost broke my promise to the stars.'

~ ◆ ~

On the seventh day Malachi threw himself into his work, and this concerned the Quasar who was had just received the first draft of their essay, and had numerous calls declined by Malachi.

On the eighth day, the North Star quit the football team and walked through the Meteorite who tried to confront him about his actions, while the Supernova had wrapped up the entire project and emailed it to the Halley's Comet.

On the ninth day, the Lonely Astronaut was moved to the recovery room and Malachi was allowed to visit her. Neither of them could bring themselves to say a word.

'You didn't break your promise.' But this did nothing to ease her conscience.

For them it wasn't the trail of broken promises they left in their wake, it was *who* they broke the promises to.

To *the stars.*
To *each other.*
To *themselves.*

Through all of this the only constants in his life were the Snapchat notifications from the Black hole who was being eaten by worry, and the silent therapy sessions.

~ ◆ ~

It had officially been a week since the Lonely Astronaut had been moved to the recovery ward. Malachi had not shed a single tear. He was steering clear of everyone around him. He fell into a pattern, driving to school with the North Star and spending most of the day with him, but not a single word was uttered. Spending the evening at the hospital with the Lonely Astronaut, the North Star and whoever decided to visit that day — where yet again not a single word was uttered.

They were healing.
They were processing.
They were gaining courage to face the world.
They were being swallowed by guilt.

Their silence was speaking for itself and their mere presence around each other was healing them.

If they could face each other, maybe... just maybe they could face the world.

~ ✦ ~

There was week left until the final assignment for Mr Salone's class, and the three groups had been given an extension, but one half of each group feared that getting in touch with their respective partners was impossible. Only emails with documents for the project were being sent. They were finishing the project but they weren't getting anywhere.

The Halley's Comet who had achieved her goal of finishing the project before her self-proclaimed rivalling captain couldn't bring herself to rub it in his face.

Everyone was spiralling. Slowly and steadily spiralling, but nobody did a good job of hiding it, because everyone else was so wrapped up in their own worries and lies they failed to notice the lies everyone else around was spewing while dodging questions.

Malachi cried on the seventeenth day and he didn't stop until the eighteenth day.

He broke.

~ ◆ ~

He didn't know what to do.
He didn't know who to turn to.
He didn't want to break his promises.

Malachi didn't know how he'd ended up here.

Alone.

Mismatched tombstones on the well-manicured green grass greeted him. The soft wind danced around him gingerly and the afternoon sun sang a song in hues of red.

The leaves danced in the soft wind, not daring to make a single sound. Malachi walked under the shade of the trees, slowly making his way to his destination.

'You looked like you were fading away.'

For the first time in his life he wasn't fading away.

He was present.

The soft rustle of every leaf, every bouquet placed at every tombstone grounded him, and so did the inscriptions on each stone, the final mark of the person.

He came to his destination, under the shade of a tree there stood a grey tombstone.

Here lies Eros Remington.
A loving son and friend.

But that wasn't all he'd left behind and that wasn't all he was.

Malachi fell to his knees and placed the bouquet near the heaviest object in the whole world. He didn't know what to say. In fact, he didn't want to say anything but he couldn't stop the words from flying out.

'I miss you,' his voice voice was scratchy and broken.

This was the first time he had spoken in the last few days.

There were so many words left unsaid, but this wouldn't be his last time here.

Coming here on its own was his first big step.

His first big step of many.

~ ✦ ~

echoing the silence

to the stars,

as it turns out we can also create bonds like characters do in books. Now i'll create memories.

~idyllically, Malachi.

The Lonely Astronaut was discharged and life was slowly going back to normal. Then again it wasn't really normal to begin with. She came to school with her coloured hair slightly faded, with a bright smile and her doctor's strict instructions, but her presence on its own relieved some of the tension in the pristine building.

The student council president was seen in meetings and helping various clubs and students.
The music had returned under the willow tree.
The football team got their goalkeeper back.

The world was slowly falling back into place and Malachi was taking his place in the shadows.

Their finals were coming up in two weeks and everyone was tense and sleep deprived. They didn't want to process their emotions and they couldn't bring themselves to do the same.

They were all just getting by.
They were all awaiting the inevitable.
They just had no idea when it would come.
And yet, here sat Malachi and the Quasar on the terrace, at the picnic tables three days before their assignment was due.

The sun had set and the fairy lights lit the terrace.

It was ethereal.

Malachi sat across the Quasar whose murky eyes were gleaming brilliantly in the light.

'So...' Malachi started trailing off even though he had come up with the idea of meeting up in the coffee shop.

She didn't say anything; she just stood up and threw herself onto him.

She hugged him.
Tightly.
Fiercely.
Warmly.

This wasn't the first time he had been hugged but there was something different about this hug that made his frozen form return the hug.

It wasn't a greeting.
It wasn't formal.
It wasn't full of pity.
It wasn't reassurance.
It wasn't... anything.

It was a hug.

As she let go of him and made her way back to her chair, Malachi found himself missing the warmth of her embrace.

'Is your social filter off or on?'
'How do you not have dark circles?' he blurted out trying to delay the inevitable.

If she is almost always awake in the dead of the night, how does she not have dark circles?

She cocked her head to the side and blinked twice.

'Huh? How-'
'You don't sleep much in the night and you still don't look like a panda.'

Her initial shock washed away and she began laughing at the boy's antics.

'So, your social filter is off.' Her mirthful comment made heat rush to his face and he leaned away from his rainbow special with extra ice.

'And to answer your question, I don't sleep. I hibernate.' She seemed satisfied with her answer and took a sip from her iced tea.

Malachi cracked a smile at her words and they soon fell into casual conversation. She thankfully did not bring up anything about their conversation from that night, nor did she mention their assignment. She was just there in the moment with him and Malachi understood why the other students hovered around her. She wasn't the sun.

She was the brightest thing in the universe and when people found her, they couldn't think of letting her go, yet alone looking away.

'It is for the baby.'
'What baby?' her eyes flashed with recognition, 'If you say you are the baby, I'm going to kick you in the face.'

Malachi smiled at her and continued drinking his second drink of the evening.

Black coffee.

'Babies can't have caffeine,' she smirked smugly and reached forward to swipe his drink.

After all, like every person, not only does darkness surround her — it also lives in her, but her bright nature burns away the shadows.

Malachi explained his plan for the project to her. Although taken aback by the drastic changes he proposed she didn't say no. They spent two days working on their project and juggling the extra work that came with it, and somehow still studied for their exams.

Malachi knew what he had to do.

After all, he didn't really have much of a choice.

~ ✦ ~

The clock in the well-disguised interrogation room claimed that it was time for the final groups to face their fate after their extension.

The Supernova and the Halley's Comet were first, followed by the Meteorite and the still-healing Lonely Astronaut, and finally, Malachi and the Quasar who had to read out their essay.

The first pair had dragged the North Star with them as a live example for their topic, which was something along the lines of food.

Malachi barely heard what the second pair spoke about because his heart was beating too loudly. He couldn't bring himself to listen yet alone go over his material. He was taking a big risk and he couldn't help but rethink his decision for making the last-minute change.

He was terrified but he didn't show it.
He watched the presentation calmly with a smile of encouragement.

When they wrapped up, Malachi and the Quasar took their place at the front of the interrogation room.

'Ms Davis and Mr Elakrab will be presenting their topic through an essay and a presentation,' Mr Salone explained while staring into the souls of his class.

The Quasar began and everyone watched eagerly at what the duo had to say.

'Our topic is People,' she paused and took a deep breath and began.

'There is so much to the topic that we didn't know where to begin so we chose to discuss what makes people shine,' she paused, 'Their calling or their passion in life.

'Something that matters the most to them,' Malachi continued, 'we soon realised how terribly wrong we were.'

The Quasar dimmed the light and presented the first slide, the picture Malachi clicked at the unconventional get-together.

This caused all those who were present in the picture to squawk and whine, but one look from Mr Salone and they shut their mouths. Even in the darkness the man was positively terrifying with his sharp black eyes that hid behind his frameless glasses and slicked back hair.

'In this picture I see people in their true element,' Malachi paused, 'even with their books and laptops open while they study or help each other or even mock each other, they feel joy just being around each other.'

'Just the mere presence of people can make a big difference,' the Quasar smiled and changed the next slide.

The next picture was one of the North Star icing cupcakes, which caused a whisper of laughter to ripple in the room.

'In this picture we see Devon baking with a smile on his face,' she smiled at the boy. 'It makes sense since this is his calling in life... but it isn't the fact that he's baking that makes him smile, it's who he is baking for.'

The next slide had a video which showed the North Star walking over to the Lonely Astronaut and the Supernova who were sitting on the floor surrounded by textbooks and pained expressions. He handed them a box which had the same cupcakes he was seen icing earlier.

The smile on his face was blinding.

'He bakes so that he can share all his emotions with the people that he cares about, without actually saying any words,' Malachi explained.

Yet another ripple of laughter ran through the class and even in the darkness Malachi could see the North Star's ears turn red.

The next slide showed a picture of the Lonely Astronaut sketching something while leaning against the bark of the Willow tree.

The slide which followed showed the same picture but at a different angle, where one could see what she was sketching. A sketch of Fire and Air gawking at the twins who were peacefully playing their respective instruments.

'Acenath only draws things that she sees potential in, but most of her sketches are of her own friends doing something mundane.' This time coos rippled through the classroom.

Just like that Malachi and the Quasar continued through the rest of their presentation.

Until a slide which had a picture of the stars was presented.

'This whole project got me thinking about my connection to people,' he paused, knowing that there was no going back now. 'We showed you pictures of Cordelia swimming, Vince playing football, Mahnoor and Nuriyah playing their instruments and random pictures of other people doing seemingly mundane things.'

'We realised that people make our universe,' the duo said together.

'Through the process of this project I was forced to talk to new people and talk to people in general,' he smiled. 'About a few months ago — I thought that my whole world had crumbled when I lost someone who meant a lot to me and I began running away from the people who were still there. I was afraid of getting hurt again.

'A Quasar helped me see through the darkness that I was drowning in.' The slide showed a picture of Talon smiling brightly at a few of her classmates and helping them with something.

'The North Star guided me when I was lost.' A picture of Devon glancing through a book while sitting on the floor of the familiar library.

'A Lonely Astronaut lost in space kept me company.' A picture of Acenath sipping a steaming hot drink while side-eyeing her laptop flashed on the slide.

'A Supernova reminded me about the beauty of the darkness.' A picture of Arthur working on a contraption of sorts in the lab was shown on the next slide.

'A Meteorite stopped me from fading away.' A picture of Vince climbing a tree flashed on the next slide.

'I found the Halley's Comet.' A picture of Cordelia pouting in the physics lab made its way onto the next slide.

'I admired the Aurora Borealis.' The picture from the night before the school festival glittered on the screen.

'I was drawn to a Black hole.' A picture of Ryoung Sae-Hee holding a fluffy white puppy flashed onto the screen.

'I was welcomed by the Elements of Nature.' A picture of René throwing her trench coat at Sebastian who was laughing made its way onto the screen, followed by one of Marco waiting for football practice to get over with Parker, while they both looked like they were going to fall asleep while standing.

'All of this made me realise that it was indeed people that make our universe and I got scared of the idea of losing them even though I'd just found them.'

There was absolute silence in the room while Talon picked up a plastic folder from which she pulled out a piece of paper. She inhaled deeply while Malachi switched on the lights giving the class a moment to adjust their eyes to the light.

'To the stars,' she began, 'I think we are drawn to pain. Drawn to everything about it because that's what connects us to people. Not love, but pain,' she smiled while reading, 'because if you feel pain you know you loved and then you lose another piece of yourself and someone loses another piece to you. In this world, pain and love go hand-in-hand and at this point we can't tell them apart,' she paused to hand the paper to Malachi who continued.

'It's because people make our universe, I selfishly thought that I could use pieces of them to replace what I had lost — but I soon came to admire what I had found. I found a universe which I'm still discovering. But it's not all darkness and light,' he sighed. 'It's more than the shades of grey in our world. I felt like I was black and white in a kaleidoscopic world of colour,' he paused. 'I was the unfinished part of this canvas, but with so many celestials around me having found their colours and calling, so can I.'

'The first thing I have to do is take a step back and absorb the light they shed into my life,' Malachi looked up. 'Then I will start taking steps fit for me to make my way back into this universe that leaves me breathless,' he smiled, 'because of the delicate love and hope which I'm nurturing — I can't close my eyes to this shining sky.'

'Idyllically, Malachi and Talon,' they concluded together.

Mr Salone smiled at the duo while the class applauded – with that the bell rang and everyone escaped the interrogation room.

~ ◆ ~

At the coffee shop Malachi couldn't get his *friends* off of him. They were dressed in clothes that bore a minute resemblance to the blue and grey uniform, clinging onto him and giving him *unwelcomed* hugs. He instantly drew the line when someone tried to kiss him.

It seemed as though after the presentation everyone wanted to drown him in affection. In fact, earlier in the day the twins decided to drop by and thank him with small hugs and encouraging words.

'I'm kinda weirded out by the fact that we didn't notice you click these pictures.' René mused while pushing her hairband up to move her hair away from her eyes.

'Yeah, you could become a photographer for one of those celebrity gossip magazines,' Marco added with a smirk of his own while bothering his helix piercing.

'I take it all back; I hate all of you.'

'Just because you are embarrassed Malachi, you don't need to lie,' Sebastian chirped, 'We know we are your universe.'

Parker laughed while his eyes gleamed behind his dark sunglasses at Malachi's plight.

'Oh, by the way who was that girl?' Talon asked, 'The Black hole?' she added helpfully.

Her question sent a rush of excitement through the group.

'Is she your girlfriend?' Vince teased while Marco turned his attention away from his sandwich and to the boy who was sipping his liquid rainbow.

He smiled while pointing at his drink for dramatic effect and watched as everyone connected the dots in their heads.

René extended her hand out to the table while Marco begrudgingly reached out for his wallet.

'You bet on that?' Cordelia sounded appalled, 'Why didn't you include me?' Her real motive was barely concealed unlike her freckles that hid behind her short hair.

'She's one of Remington's friends,' he turned to Acenath who was on Vince's screen and Devon. 'She was the one who mailed out the letters.'

They nodded in acknowledgement while Malachi choked on his next sip when recognition flashed in his eyes and fumbled for his phone. He opened the app, and readied the camera while getting up to get everyone in the picture.

'Smile,' he called.

'Vince lift me up!!' Acenath yelled and the boy fumbled with his phone bringing it up.

Malachi clicked the picture and before sending it as a streak to Sae-Hee, he took a brief moment to admire the scene before him.

Both René and Talon had flashed bright smiles. René however made sure to cover Marco's face with her hand. The boy in the overalls with various piercings on his ear, was too invested in his sandwich to notice the trench coat-clad arm blocking his face. Parker smiled over his cup of coffee while Sebastian hooked his arm over Vince's shoulder, who was fumbling with his phone which had Acenath posing dramatically on the other end of the call. Devon who was sitting across them had seemed to notice this, and began cackling at Vince's plight while Arthur who sat by the cackling boy's side looked at all of them with a fond smile, and his tattoo was out for the world to see. Cordelia was sitting cross-legged slightly away from the chaos, with her own phone out and snapping a picture of the chaotic bunch that surrounded her.

They all sat on the picnic table under the umbrellas at the terrace on their own personal vacation, taking a break from their looming exams.

Malachi sending the picture resulted in her almost instantly sending him an array of messages, each with a different tone and context.

'Did you take a screenshot of the previous snap?'
'You took a screenshot but you won't reply to me?'

'Are you okay?'
'Now you reply.'
'You killed our streak!'
'Are those your friends?'
'What happened?'
'Tell me later, have fun with your friends now.'

He smiled at his screen.

I'm going to be okay.

~ ✦ ~

'I told you so,' she practically sang when he began playing the piano.
'Hello to you too Kamaria.'

She smirked at him, 'To what do I owe the pleasure?' she asked while
joining him.
'I'm graduating next week.'
'Wow,' she sighed.
'I know, I'm just as surprised if not more,' he laughed tipping his head
back slightly.

'How've you been?' she asked.
'I'm getting there.'
'That's nice.'

'So, *Stardust*,' he smiled at her.

She made a face at him and he smiled fondly at her with a dim light
in his eyes.

'Do you know how I met Eros?'
'No, why?' she asked tilting her head in confusion.

Though neither of them was surprised with her reaction, after all,
Malachi usually played the piano when he was overwhelmed, so the
girl with the slightly fading tattooed on her arm had never seen the
mundane and bright aspects of his life.

'Our school had taken us to the planetarium and we were divided
into groups,' he explained. 'He was in my group even though he was
a year older than me — let me tell you for a six-year-old he sure had
an attitude,' he said with a fond and wistful smile. 'He ended up with
myself, Acenath and Devon.'

She stopped playing and turned to look at him. 'He deemed himself
group leader since he was older and spoke like he was eighty.'
'Weren't your parents working together? I though he was your family

friend?' she asked tilting her head.

'Not yet he wasn't, our parents began working together when I turned ten.'

She nodded her head and beckoned him to continue.

'We were being explained the concept of stars and how they actually don't twinkle.' His statement caused her to raise an eyebrow at him.

'Your school took you to the planetarium to destroy the basis of a nursery rhyme?' She squawked indignantly.

'Well no — but I think that was their goal,' he held a note. 'As a very passionate five-year-old I yelled out my own theory ignoring the scientific facts laid before me,' he paused. 'I theorised that what if they were actually telling us the secrets of the universe in the form of Morse Code?'

The barefoot girl let out a melodic honeyed laugh.

'I'm glad you found it funny but the guide was highly unimpressed but smiled nonetheless and explained the whole thing to me all over again,' he smiled wistfully, 'however, Eros was very impressed with my idea and the four of us spent the rest of the excursion discussing theories about the stars.'

'Conspiracy theorist at five and six, nice,' she chortled.

'Any which ways,' he rolled his eyes. 'Somehow, we came up with a new theory, that not only do they whisper the secrets of the universe but can also listen to your secrets and promises.' He paused, 'So basically if I were to promise the stars to never eat cookies...'

'You would do that?'
'No,' Malachi looked scandalized, 'this is a hypothetical situation. So, hypothetically if I were to—which I'm not—promise the stars that I were to never eat cookies they'd hear the promise,' he heaved a sigh at her dumbfounded expression. 'Which means that the others would also hear the secret.'
'Oh!'

'Yeah, but as we got older reality knocked us down but we kept on promising the stars as a sentimental thing and to show our sincerity.'
'That's cute,' she hummed, 'is that why you say *'To the stars'*?'

Malachi nodded.

'And that is why are you are stardust.'
'Huh?'
'Remnants of sincerity, precious memories, and a constant in outer space.'
'That's lame.'

Malachi glared at her but her glossy eyes told him a whole other story.

'Whatever you say, space dust.'

She was a part of him that he never wanted to let go.

~ ✦ ~

right now, is where i belong

to the stars,

we don't really exist and none of us are really unique, and yet we still fall into a pattern. a seemingly random pattern which solely exists to keep us all together and still far apart. certain times we do fall into place more than the norm dictates and these are deemed feats of wonder and miracles.

as of recently i have befriended a few, rather interesting people who have unknowingly (they know now) changed my life; well them – and the ones that i pushed away.

i get why they made a difference in my life; they all came in unapologetically as themselves which pulled me towards them, they walked into my life as things that i didn't even know I needed.

they pulled me in and kept me from falling apart, well technically i had already fallen apart, but they just kept my fragments from blowing away.

~idyllically, Malachi.

~ ✦ ~

'I now present to you the 75th graduating class of Noctem Arch Academy.'

Malachi's heart was beating out of his chest and he couldn't stop smiling just like everyone else around him. Megawatt smiles were plastered onto their faces and they couldn't help but squeal and jump in absolute joy. For the first time, everyone was dressed uniformly in the deep blue gowns and caps from which dangled their silver tassels.

Acenath and Devon ran over to him and the trio began jumping about and celebrating the closing of a major chapter in their lives. Arthur soon joined, sporting his own megawatt smile and glossy eyes.

They all had glossy eyes.

Talon was squealing and bounding from person to person as she made her way to the others. Cordelia and Vince were laughing at Marco who was constantly tripping over his own gown and René was holding back her tears while absorbing the scene around her. Parker was hiding his glossy eyes behind his sunglasses, while him and Sebastian were talking about a mile a minute about the most random things in the world.

None of them could believe this had finally happened.

After watching their seniors move on to new chapters in their lives the lot of them were getting impatient and desperate to move forward, but now that the moment had come, they were scared. Scared of growing apart and becoming memories, but with the smiles painted on their faces they pushed those thoughts away and smiled for the flashing cameras of the proud parents and teachers, who if anything, felt relived.

'AAHHHHHHH!!' Acenath yelled.

The others laughed at the girl with the plastered left arms antics but understood her feelings.

~ ✦ ~

They were at the beach with wistful smiles staring out into the waters that softly struck the sand. The wind danced around them and trees swayed gently under the moonlight. Everything about their surroundings was perfect but there were voices dancing around. In *all* of their minds.

Will we keep in touch?

I don't want to lose my friends because of a time-zone.
I — I don't want to say goodbye.

This isn't goodbye.
This is… this is until we meet again.
When will the again come?

Yeah!! Our friendship will survive… right?
Why didn't I befriend them earlier?

… This can't be it.

They hadn't known each other for long enough and that was slowly killing them, they were still mysteries to each other and this 'until we meet again' had come too quickly.

They wanted to freeze time and live in the lapsing of memories... they didn't want their bonds to fade into memories. How long until they started missing calls and soon birthday wishes? How long until they slipped away?

~ ✦ ~

To the stars,

Now that the chaotic whirlwind of the last few months of hell have passed, I finally have time to process it. In those fleeting moments of reminiscing I find myself lost and confused.

I don't know where I stand in this world or if I even have a place here. My whole life I took comfort in looking at the adults around me and figured that I too would eventually find my place in this world.

But now that everyone around me has their whole life planned out, and I feel hopeless. When did everyone figure everything out? I know that even the most fool-proof plans can fall apart… but at least they have plans.

None of us have the answers and we probably never will, after all, where is the fun in knowing everything? All I want to know is if I make it through. I don't mind making mistakes along the way — who is perfect and what good is a story with no highs and lows? I'm looking forward to making memories.

~The Lonely Astronaut.

To the stars,

This reality was a distant dream lifetimes away, and now that it's here, I can't help but feel proud of the me that closed his eyes yesterday, and I'm happy with the way things turned out even though this journey tore me apart.

The guilt of not being enough is not eating me away anymore and I feel whole again. After all I know what comes next and I know that it won't be easy but when has it ever been? I want to be able to tell the me of lifetimes away about the brilliant sky that greets me now and the celestials that adorn it.

The hues and lights that surround me bring me comfort and I can't help but want to lay here forever... but I have a long way to go and until then, I will find my strength in the sky's glittering embrace.

~ The North Star.

To the stars,

I'm looking forward to the chaos that surrounds me even after being surrounded by it for over seven years. I love it because in the chaos I found myself. Sometimes I feel like a candle that has lost her wick but I will shine. This chaos is comforting, and even though there are times it gets too much, I still find it thrilling.

This is it and I love everything about it, but every now and then I wish I could relive my memories. I miss living in a world that fit in the palm of my hand. The world which I grew up in and the people who I do not want to grow apart from.

I don't want them to fade to memories.

~The Quasar

To the stars,

Is this it? I always thought that there would be more, I guess I hoped it would be magical and I would find my place while making sense of everything that had happened in my life… almost like a fog would be lifted and things would make sense again.

Is this it? This is the anticlimactic ending to the last 22 years of my life? I'm moving to a bigger world of which I've barely scratched the surface, but why does everything feel so… cold? What am I missing?

Is this it, because I am terrified. I don't know what is happening and my instinct is to control the chaos around me, but I find myself going along with the changes and I'm okay with that. I lived in fear of the unknown and now I am lost… but I'm not terrified and that scares me more but I'll be okay because I know what I have to do in this world.

~ The Supernova.

To the stars,

The road was in no way easy but now that I stand here, I know it was worth it. I'm going to miss the days where my eyes were practically glued shut and I wasn't the only zombie in a 5-mile radius. I miss the comfort those days carried with them.

I live in the realm of stable instability where I have my legs planted on the ground, after 6 years I'd like to think I got the hang of it, but with the cyclones that are a part of my life, I don't have absolute faith in my legs and I wouldn't change it for the world.

Every day I meet someone better, stronger, smarter or faster... and I can't help but wonder if I am enough to be running the same race as them but then again, I have the cyclonic celestials that still run circles around me reminding me of what we were and who we have to become.

~The Meteorite.

To the stars,

I never thought the world outside of water would be this comforting and chaotic, yet here I am in a world that I can accept myself in. My heart still belongs to the water but I'm happy in this world that I stumbled into.

A project that was given too much importance opened the doors to this world where the sun never rises and the people revel in the darkness that gleams for them. I didn't get bored of them and they didn't get tired of me.

Even though it has been years, I can't help but wonder what would have happened if we hadn't spoken? The stars would have merely been gas giants, light years away, and I would have just been Cordelia Delta Blue.

~The Halley's Comet.

To the stars,

The sun has set on another year and with it, I rise to face the next year. Every year I find myself yearning to relive the past… so that we could have had more time but the memories we leave in our wake are good enough.

I wish I could tell my yesterday's self that all those dreams are now a reality but I had to work harder for them than I had ever anticipated. I wouldn't be here had it not been for the hope they set ablaze in me when I couldn't see the light.

I'm here and it's perfect.

~Fire.

To the stars,

We lived lifetimes in a decade and now we stand at the edge. I don't know what this new chapter marks but I'm ready for it.

I look forward to it and I look forward to unknowingly making memories that will live on forever.

Now at the edge, I can say that I am ready to take that leap.

~Earth.

To the stars,

I still don't understand why I write these letters, and in all honesty, I don't think I want to stop. It keeps the inner child in me alive and without that who am I?

A simple thank you won't suffice to this tradition which at this point is a habit which held us all together even though the odds were stacked against us.

~ Air.

To the stars,

I'm finally good enough and I'm happy with the result.

Being good enough was a long shot but to be happy with the result itself was unrealistic but, I'm here now. I made it. Step-by-step and each step made for me because I have to be good enough for myself and not for the rest of the world which in its own way, is perfect.

~Water.

darkness

feel.

~ ✦ ~

I'm screaming and shouting,
My heart is burning.
I'm leaning into the darkness; I can feel it calling.
It keeps on pulling.

Darkness, here I am again. Getting roped in.
Walking into your depths with my eyes wide open.
I can see through your lies.
I can hear their cries.

Their eyes full of fear and a dying flame.
Hope is our final aim.
The cold fire within grows.
We'll keep you on your toes.

Yet another victim falls from the stars.
Victory will be ours.
We won't be yours to keep,
We'll take that leap.

The skies will light up as we rise.
I'm tired of your lies.
I'll take them away I swear.
The stars will have their prayer.

~ ✦ ~